Stock Market Swing Trading

The Definitive Guide to anticipate market moves through the signals of Technical and Fundamental Analysis. How to generate Passive Income disciplining your emotional decisions.

Table of Contents

1. Introduction:

Picture this: you're in your house, sitting and sulking in your bed, hoping there was so much more you could do with your life. You want to go travel to Budapest or Uzbekistan, or maybe you want to go get a diploma from that culinary school in Malaysia, but unfortunately, you can't. You just can't seem to afford it. The common factor for all that you desire in this world is the need for money.

But you could turn your life around. You could continue to sit at your home, but make such smart trading decisions that with the click of a few buttons, financing your dreams is something you never have to worry about ever again. Of course, despite what some people might have you believe, trading will not give you overnight success, unless you have exceptional luck. I mean, if you were to gamble away $50,000 and by the end of the night you made $250,000, you increased your wealth through an incredibly risky trade, but continuing to do this is not a sound plan. Similarly, trading is beyond risky, and if you don't make calculated and educated decisions, rather than profiting in millions, you could be wiping away all your account assets and applying for a mortgage instead, making you worse off. But have no fear, we are here to tell you all the basics you need to know to get started on trading, and more specifically, 'Swing Trading.'

Before getting into the details of what swing trading is, and how one must go about it to profit from it, it is important to first try to understand the concept of trading itself. When a layman thinks of 'trading,' the mind goes back to the good old days when individuals used to barter. After all, that is where everything economics-related originated from. Before money ever even came into play, people directly exchanged commodities, whether they were goods or services, in order to get commodities in return. And if not that, then the mind goes to international trade, where countries export goods and services with other countries, in order to get a good deal and hence, import the goods and services that they in turn require. In both these concepts, the common denominator is a 'transfer of goods or services' from one entity, whether it's a person or a country, to another entity. Barter incorporated a direct exchange of goods and services for other goods and services, whereas international trade occurs via money. Trade is a basic concept of economics, and we see it around us every day. You go to the market, and you see people exchanging money in order to get good. You do it yourself when you go to the store and get your groceries for the month. It is a common practice and essential to our everyday life. As a buyer, if you pay enough *compensation* to the seller, you can get whatever goods or services you require.

The compensation, referred to above, is usually money. As a medium of exchange, money facilitates the trade of all kinds in today's world. Money itself alone does not hold any value. It is some of its attributes and functions that allow for it to be worth so much. *"Money is a function of four: A medium; a measure; a standard; and a store."* This means that money has four basic functions, as listed and explained below:

1. **A Medium of Exchange:** A primary function of money, as a medium of exchange it facilitates transactions to occur. The major problem with the barter system of trade was that obtaining a particular commodity from a supplier was complicated because it was difficult to possess a commodity of equal value that the supplier would have also desired. There had to be a *'double coincidence of wants,'* whose occurrence was very unlikely. This is why money was introduced. It completely eliminates the dilemma by serving as a medium of exchange, as money is accepted by all parties in every transaction;

2. **The measure of Value:** As aforementioned, it was hard to find goods with equal value to exchange in the barter system. This function of money removed that difficulty by serving as a common measure of value. All goods and services have their value expressed in terms of price, which is in term expressed with money;

3. **Standard of Deferred Payment:** This function allows money to be borrowed and lent. Deferred payments are such that can be postponed for the future, enabling current transactions to be made later on in times yet to come;

4. **Store of Value:** Being a store of value allows money to be used as a means of saving because it causes this medium to be a repository of purchasing power over time. In simple words, from the time it is received to the time it is spent, money is used to save purchasing power because it more or less retains its values, at least retains its value the most as compared to other assets like bonds.

The reason all this about money is being explained to you is that these functions will play a vital role in helping you understand how trading works, because everything about trading is oriented around money, and how well you know how to spend and invest your money.

Moving on, the network or system that allows for trade to exist is known as a market. There are many different types of markets in the world. There is the basic goods/commodities market, also known as the consumer market. This should be self-explanatory. It is the market where goods and services are sold. Then there is also the job market, or more commonly known as the labor market, where households supply labor and firms demand it; where jobs are done in return for wages. Then, as we have already established, there is also the global/international market, which deals with imports and exports between countries. The market we will be talking about, however, is in a league of its own: The Stock Market.

The Stock Market is where investors, such as you, would go to buy and sell investments, also known as stocks. These investments are essentially shares of ownership in a public company, formulating a sort of partnership between the company and the shareholder. Still, confused? Don't understand what shares are and how they work? Let me explain. All publically traded, and even some privately held firms have shares. A share is a piece, or unit, of ownership that a person has in the firm. It is a financial instrument that represents ownership in a corporation.

Each company has a fixed legally authorized quantity of shares that they are allowed to distribute, and people can buy those shares from the company. Once you buy a share, you become a shareholder. This means the company has to provide you with the equity, i.e., in a way, their profit (total liabilities deducted from their total assets) in that company. The share you own represents a proportionate claim on the company's earnings. As a shareholder, you become entitled to a percentage of profits that were made by the company, because you own a small part of that company. One example to clarify this would be that if you owned 100,000 shares of a firm that had one million outstanding shares, all the shares of a corporation that were authorized, you would have 10% ownership of the company. These payments made to the shareholder by the company are referred to as dividends. When you buy a share, they can be sold further on in physical or virtual 'stock' exchanges. You may be wondering though, why does a company even issue shares? Why give out your profits? Well, this is because in this fast-paced economy, where every firm has competition left, right, and center, company's require access to large sums of financial capital. To bring forth their ideas in the form of product, there are many costs a firm must bear, such as transportation logistics, getting equipment and materials, paying labor, and much, much more. These costs can only be boring if the firm has enough finances in their pockets. Raising capital can be done in two ways: selling shares or borrowing money. Selling shares end up being the preferred route for most firms because financing debts can end up being more costly due to interest. This way, when individuals 'buy' shares, they are providing the company with capital, which further helps the company to earn profits.

The stock market is the market where *our kind of trading* occurs. The trading you and I are interested in, the one we want to learn in order to make passive income. It is where we trade shares. The simplest way to think of trading in the stock market is to think of its terms of buying. In trading terminology, this is known as 'Going Long.'

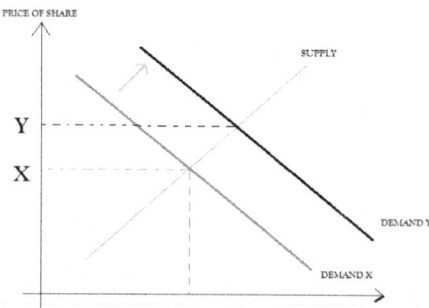

Figure 1: Rise in Demand leads to an Increase in Market Price

Source 1: own-sourced

You buy a share at a price 'X,' and hold onto your position. To hold your position means to neither buy nor sell the share, but to rather hold onto it. You would do this because your gut feeling, or maybe lots of research, told you that the market for the share you bought is going to rise, meaning the company's profits are going to go up, and more people will want to have shares from that company.

This rise in demand for the share pushes the price up to 'Y,' at which you sell the share you had previously bought, making a nice amount of profit for yourself.

Besides, there being different strategies of trading, trading itself has two portfolio managing strategies:

1. Active Trading; and
2. Passive Trading.

In active trading, a trader buys and sells their stocks and shares based on short term movements. This is done in order to profit from price movements shown on a short-term stock chart. A stock chart is very simply a chart that plots down all the prices of a stock over a certain time period. The stock chart also has a lot of other information on it, such as the symbol of a stock, which is a unique series of letters given to the stock to describe it, and the chart also states which specific exchange it trades on. It is believed by active traders that capturing the market is where profits are made. Passive trading is a low cost, low maintenance and low-risk form of investing, and such traders are those who follow a 'Buy and Hold' strategy where they buy stocks and shares for long periods of times, such as a few months or even a few years, despite the fluctuations in the market. 'Buy and Hold' is more applicable to investments rather than trading, but it is often used by some traders as a method to hold on to stocks as well. Any stock that is bought for a year it automatically categorizes as an investment, but some traders in the market just prefer to keep their investment and trading portfolio separate.

The passive trader tracks the market index, which measures price changes of different specified groups of stocks, whereas the active trader tries to beat the market by making quick but smart, calculated, and confident risks. If an active trader successfully beats the market, they end up making higher than average returns, because of the higher risk they were involved in. The kind of trading you choose to do depends on your psychological makeup and personality. If you are one who gets anxious and stressed very quickly, and cannot deal with fast-paced trading that could make you lose just as much as it would help you gain, active trading is not the one for you. The relaxed nature of passive trading would connect with your frequency more, and it is also a more affordable way to access the market. You can use passive trading to get a hold of trading, and then switch to active trading when you're more confident with your decisions. In the long run, if you want to make quick money, active trading is the way to go about it, and even the market for active trading is vaster, as not a lot of products are available that suit the passive approach.

Besides active trading and the 'Buy and Hold' approach, there is also what is known as 'Positional Trading.' Active trading is short term, while 'Buy and Hold' is long term. Positional Trading is, on the other hand, a medium-term method. The time duration is neither in days or years, but rather months.

This all may seem daunting to a beginner, but trust me when I say you are not alone. Everyone feels a bit overwhelmed and scared at first. Even I did when I had very limited experience in stocks and stock investing, but with time once you get the hang of the basic concepts and the crux of trading, and when you approach everything in a disciplined manner, it is one of the most efficient techniques to increase your net worth.

Now that the basics of trading our discussed, let us move onto the different ways one can trade.

2. What is the Swing Trading and how it Works:

The fundamental of swing trading and the difference respect the other styles of trading.

You may want to get as much knowledge as quickly as possible and might even think of skipping through this text, jumping directly to the tips and tricks of swing trading, but it would be unwise to do so. The one thing you must understand about trading is that it is pertinent to never be hasty, and especially to never rush into making decisions. Patience is a virtue, and the first step of learning trading is to patiently go through everything explained in this book, to really dive into understanding how to become one of the top-notch traders of the world. If you cannot be successfully patient here, don't expect to do well in real-life trading either. So, before getting into the vast topic of how one can become a 'Swing Trader,' it is important to first understand what Swing Trading even is, and why and how it is better than the other forms of trading.

There are various methods and strategies that allow you to accomplish trading. It comes in many forms, each having its own appropriate market environment and, of course, risks. Swing trading is a strategy for the active trading form of managing your portfolio.

Essentially with each cycle of buying and selling, your slate is clean as it contains no carryover. As already established, in active trading, you buy and sell your stocks based on the short term, which is why swing trading techniques are of short-term investing. The 'buy and hold' mantra does not apply like in that of passive investing.

Swing traders look for trends, and when new trends break. This is because, at the end of any trend, the price is very volatile. As that trend is trying to 'establish' itself, where either people will accept the trend or reject it, demand more of it, or refuse to jump on the bandwagon, the price keeps fluctuating until, with time, the decision about a trend is made by the public. As the price volatility is settling down, whether it is rising or falling, swing traders buy or sell their shares. But what is a swing?

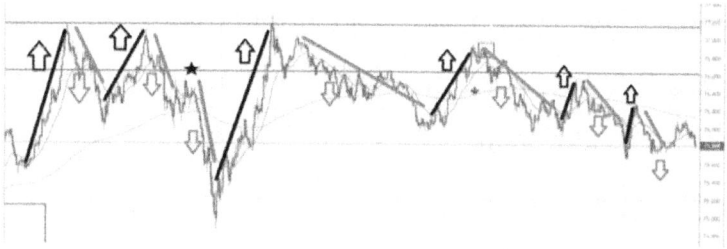

Figure 2: Ups and Downs representing 'Swings' from an Active Trader's Perspective

Source 2: own-sourced

Look at Figure 2. You can see in this chart that the price goes up, then down, then up again. This is what swings are. They have clearly marked out pivot points from which you can see either price falls or price rises. Swing trading essentially makes use of these swings and tries to capture the ones going up, as they will bring in profits. The trader's aim is to capture the swing that is most likely to happen, relevant to the shares he has or is planning to buy.

The point marked with a 'star' in 'figure 2' cannot be labeled as a swing, though. This is specifically because that particular movement has a lot of retracements happening in it on the upside and the downside. It is fluctuating too much to be labeled as a swing, and the trend is not clear.

As this segment is a comparison with other styles of trading, let's try to understand how these 'short-term' swings differentiate from 'medium-term' swings and 'long term' trading very briefly.

Positional trading is, as discussed, when a trader makes a direct call on the market, holding on to their positions for a few weeks up to a few months. Unlike in active trading, in positional trading, the trader's outlook towards his stock is not affected by the day-to-day volatility that occurs in the market.

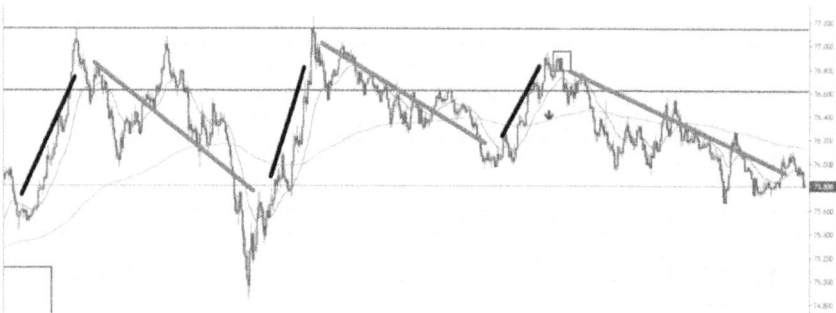

Figure 3: Swings from a Positional Trader's Perspective
Source 3: own-sourced

The positional trader is more concerned with the larger price movements, in simple words, spanning from one month to another. These larger moves are preferred by a trader of this type because he likes to get into and hold onto such kinds of positions. Swing trading and Positional Trading are more or less based on the same concepts, with the only difference being the time duration of the trade.

The 'Buy and Hold' approach looks at everything as a whole and does not really focus too much on the specifics of price rises and falls. Such a trader would not focus on swings but would hold onto his shares for large sums of time.

He would not exit on the next downturn but would keep his shares, looking at the larger picture, in hopes that conditions will become better later on.

Moving on, a swing trader holds on to their positions for two days, or even up to ten or twenty days, it all depends on the trader's preference and their psychological makeup. The crux of it, though, is that positions aren't held for long periods of time. By using algorithms and rules, via the Technical or even the Fundamental Analysis (discussed later on) such as earning projections, swing traders determine when the price will be lowest, buy them, and then sell their shares as the prices rise. This occurs more specifically when major stock events occur, such as stock market crashes or corrections, or even around *earning seasons*. Earning seasons are those months during which the majority of the quarterly corporate earnings are brought forth to the public, generally occurring in the months immediately after the end of each fiscal quarter, which is July, October, January, and April. Fiscal quarters are three-month periods in a fiscal year, which essentially is a year for finance-related objectives, referred to for accounting and even taxing purposes. It starts on the 1st of July every year, ending on the 30th of June.

The government and different corporations use the fiscal calendar to release budgets and corporate earnings. Swing traders use the information release during these 'earning seasons' to make decisions on what stocks to buy and sell, and when.

Besides Swing Trading and Positional Trading, there are two more strategies of trading as well, known as:

1. Day Trading; and
2. Scalping.

Day trading is one of the most well-known styles of active trading. As the name actually implies, in this strategy, traders buy and sell their trades within the same day, with no position being held overnight. Due to the high risks that entail this form of trading, it is taken up only by professionals: those that are specialists in their trade, or those who are Market Makers. Market Makers are individuals who deal with stocks and shares buy undertaking to buy and sell at particular prices at all times. They provide bids (offers made by the trader so that he may buy a stock) and also provide asks (a price that the seller is willing to accept for a stock). (Majaski, 2020)[1] This is done so as to profit off of the 'bid-ask spread,' the amount by which the 'ask' price surpasses the 'bid' price for a stock.

---

[1] Majaski, C. (2020, Maech 27). Day Trading vs. Swing Trading: What's the Difference? Retrieved from Investopedia:

It is the difference between the greatest price willing to be paid by the buyer, and the lowest price willingly accepted by the seller. It is, in a way, the supply, represented by the 'ask,' and demand, represented by the 'bid' for a particular stock, showing how liquid the stock is. This brings us to the last type of strategy, as well: Scalping.

Considered to be one of the quickest strategies, even quicker than day trading, scalpers exploit the price gaps that occur due to the 'bid-ask spreads.' They buy at the bid price and sell at the asking price, inheriting the difference between these two price points. There is the least amount of risk associated with this strategy, as scalpers hold onto their positions for very short periods of time so as to make sure they don't face a change in the spread which they chose to buy their assets from. Scalpers do not exploit large moves. Since they move smaller volumes, they search for more liquid markets, as the more liquidity a stock has, the greater its 'bid-ask spread.' (Bajpai, 2019)[2]

The type of trading strategy that is best for you is all dependent upon the kind of personality you have, what kind of risks you are willing to take, and whether you have the patience or not.

---

https://www.investopedia.com/articles/active-trading/052815/pros-cons-day-trading-vs-swing-trading.asp

[2] Bajpai, P. (2019, August 8). Scalping vs. Swing Trading: What's the Difference? Retrieved from Investopedia: https://www.investopedia.com/articles/active-trading/021715/scalping-vs-swing-trading.asp

Look at the table below, which is a quick comparison in different aspects between all the four types of active trading measures discussed:

	Scalp Trading	Day Trading	Swing Trading	Position Trading
Holding	Few Seconds to Few Minutes	A Day at most, Never overnight	Few days to Few Weeks	Few Weeks to a Few Months
Quantity of Trades	Few – Hundred during the day	1 – 5 Trades a Day	1 – 5 trades a Month	1 – 3 in a span of a Few Months
Trader's Personality	Impatient Traders, Vigilant Traders	Impatient Traders with less time on their hand	Patient Traders, Good Trend Analysts	Patient Traders, Easy Going Traders
Decision Making	Rapid	Quick	Fluid	You can take your time
Stress	Very High	High	Moderate	Low
Strategy	Extreme	Extreme	Moderate	Moderate
Suitability	Professionals	Semi-Professional, Passionate	Suitable for All	Suitable for All
Tracking Period	Constant Monitoring	Constant Monitoring	Reasonable Monitoring, remain up-to-date on the news, change in policies, stock events	Reasonable Monitoring
Charts to Refer to	Tick Charts/1-5 Minute Charts	415 Tick Charts, Day Charts	Daily/Weekly Charts	Monthly Charts
Profit	Multiple, but Small	Average	Large, but Few	Few

Table 1: Comparison between different active trading strategies

On smaller accounts, day trading and scalping have much higher profit potential. Position trading can you give you large sums of profits at a single time, but take a really long time to do so. This is why Swing Trading is one of the best methods of trading, most bound to give you the best chances to succeed. It is the perfect balance between the different extremes and is bound to give you the least amount of stress. Even though day trading may give quick profits, it also entails lots of losses in trades. For a novice, at least, day trading is a foo's game that will suck you into it by triggering the impatient and greedy trait we all have to make quick and fast money. Like I mentioned before, patience is the key to success in the game of trading, which is why one should opt for Swing Trading. With position trading, you may get good payoffs as you retire, if you want to become an avid trader, and be one of the best in the game, this method will not do you much good either.

Swing trading is not only the perfect balance, but with it, you can also fit in your trading around whatever busy schedule you may have. (Fuller, 2016)[3] You can go about your normal life while continuing to make money on the side to be able to make that vacation next time you get a few holidays or fulfill any other dream you had, which seemed impossible before because of a lack of finance. You can analyze the market on your own terms, without having to rush to see what event has taken place next. Not only this, but it is also important to not overcomplicate your trading by being involved all the time. For a chance at success, it is important to be slightly less involved and make fewer trades over time, which swing trading will entail. It prevents you from over-trading, one of the major reasons people lose so much of their money. You should make sure to not become addicted to trading.

---

[3] Fuller, N. (2016, February 26). Why Swing Trading Gives You The Best Chance to Succeed. Retrieved from Learn to Trade the Market: https://www.learntotradethemarket.com/forex-trading-strategies/best-swing-trading-strategy

3. First Step for Beginners and Insightful tips for Experienced Traders:

Explication, step by step, for becoming a swing trader. Enrichment of proven knowledge for experienced traders.

Swing Trading is quite a vast topic, making it difficult for a lot of beginners, however, I will try to simplify it as much as possible to make this strategy as simple as possible for you.

As we have established, the main strategy of swing trading is to 'capture' different swings. But how do these swings work, and when should a trader buy or sell stocks based on the different trends of the price of stocks. For that, let's understand the 'Structure Support and Resistance.'

Structure Support and Resistance:
Look at Figure 4. The waves represent 'swings.' Initially, as the index of stock prices rises, it reaches point 'A.' Point 'A' is a turning point, after which the price fell.

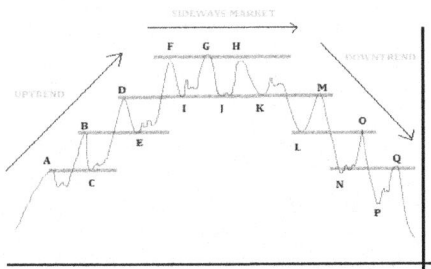

Figure 4: Depiction of Support and Resistance Levels

Source 4: own-sourced

22

At this point, the resistance level is established. It is essentially a level from which rejects a further increase in price. The price falls again, but due to some market changes, the prices start to rise, due to the upward trend of prices, and eventually breaks out through the resistance level at point 'A'. The new resistance level is established at the turning point 'B', with the old resistance level automatically becoming the support level for the price changes, preventing prices from further falling, working as floor. This constant turnover of support and resistance levels is common in upward and downward trends. When the trend becomes sideways, where turning points are more or less around the same points, the support and resistance level remains constant.

When looking at the figure, points 'F', 'G', and 'H' make up the resistance level, while points 'I', 'J', and 'K' make up the support level. In a sideways market, the price trend keeps moving within the two levels, not breaking through either. Eventually, though, if the price level breaks out from the support level and falls when it goes back up, the previous 'floor' now becomes the 'roof', preventing price from exceeding that level. This formulates a downward trend in the market. As this continues, points 'L' and 'N', which made up the support levels alternate to become the resistance levels at points 'O' and 'Q'.

These levels aren't just lines but are areas around which you can see the corrective movie of the stock prices.

Before moving on, let's label each point in Figure 4:

→ A/B/D= Higher-High;

→ C/E = Higher-Low;

→ L/N/P = Lower-Low;

→ M/O/Q = Lower-High.

You can profit off both uptrends and downtrends in swing trading. In an uptrend, where you have to capture the swings that moving in the upward direction, you search for the 'High-Lows.'

During the downtrend, where the main aim to capture swings going down, you search for the 'Lower-Highs.' In an uptrend, after determining the 'Higher-Lows,' it is at those points that you buy your stocks, while in a downtrend, you sell at the 'Lower-Highs' that have been determined to get good returns on your trading. This is because, after 'Higher-Lows,' the price rises so when you eventually decide to sell it, you'll make profits, and after 'Lower-Highs,' the price falls, so selling at these points is most beneficial if you want to get the maximum money in return, as after this the price will get lower and lower, reducing your profit margins.

In a sideways market, you can both buy and sell at any point you deem worthy, but the upward and downward trend has specific rules as to when you should buy or sell in order to have a successful trade. While Swing Trading, the positions held normally are held from two days to ten or even twenty days. It all depends on the trends and the trader's personal preference. It is pertinent to search for high probability trades and to take part in them, so as to make high rewards. As a beginner, though, you should aim for low-risk trades so that you get the hang of the basics first, and if you make losses, they do not affect your finances too much.

Now, let's discuss different swing trading strategies that will help you become successful in the financial market, no matter what you are trading with, whether it is Stocks or even other assets such as Futures and Options, it all applies in the same manner, but we will only focus on stocks in our current discussion.

The first and foremost is known as the 'Catch the Wave' strategy. It is important to capture the swings that are in line with the trend, as those moves are much stronger. Essentially, it is suggested to exit the trade and sell your stocks just before the swing high or swing low, as after prices are determined to fall or rise, respectively. The main focus is to decide the decision before the opposing trend occurs.

Then there is the 'Stuck in a Box' strategy. This is for when the price is stuck in a range, as it usually is in a sideways market. In such a market, you let the price reach the support level. You wait for the price trend to be rejected as buyers enter the market, pushing the price up. When the price is pushed up a little, you buy your stocks at that point, as after it, the price is expected to rise to the resistance level that you identify. At that point, you can sell your stock.

The next strategy is known as 'Fade the Move' and is very important for swing traders to know of. Although it is more aggressive in nature, as it is a counter-trend trade, if executed correctly, it offers a favorable risk to reward ratio. It is a high-risk strategy, deployed by professional traders who are stuck after they went relatively long because of a wrong prediction of market trends. Let us assume that in a market that is generally in an uptrend, the price hit a support level, and then starts to rise again. Taking into account previous trends, you assume it will break out through the resistance level, but instead, the market collapses at that level, reverses and takes a downturn.

The traders assumed the market would go higher, but instead, it reversed and took a 180-degree turn. So, in a manner of counter trading, as you are trading against the trend, you go short and sell your stocks after capturing a single downwards swing, exiting the trade, as you do not want to overstay your welcome. Another strategy is that of 'Spread Betting.' It is a derivative one, in which traders essentially are unaware of the underlying stocks they have bet on, but rather speculate on whether the price of the stock will rise or fall, by referring to the prices offered to them by a broker. If placed correctly, spread betting can yield very high profits.

However, this is a method more effective for traders with lots of experience and knowledge, as they understand the trends more and know-how and when to take risks. In some countries, profits earned from spread betting are also tax-free, like in the United Kingdom. Similar to this method is the Contract for Difference (CFD) as well, another popular form of derivative trading. It enables you to speculate on the price rises and falls for fast-moving global stock markets, without having to take ownership of underlying shares. It involves a trader and a bank, and at the end of the contract, both the parties exchange the difference between the 'bid' and 'ask' price of the stock.

However, CFD is considered to be quite risky and is also illegal in some countries, such as in the United States of America.

To be a good swing trader, you must make use of both the Fundamental and Technical Analysis, whether you're a novice or an experienced trader. Never assume that you know everything. Constantly do a market overview to get a gist of new trends that could occur due to various reasons, whether it is an innovated product, like the Electric Car release for Tesla, or if it's a major stock event like a natural disaster hitting an economy, the first task of the day should be to catch up on the latest news and developments of the market.

4. The Most Suitable Financial Instruments for Swing Trading:

Stock market and swing trading: which are the best types of shares and options for trading with charts and examples

Considering the fact that swing trading is a short term method, where quick thinking and decision making is required, the financial instrument you choose is highly pivotal, along with which chart you look at, how to formulate your own pattern and how to use your knowledge to make the correct decisions.

First, let us understand what the Stock Market is and how it functions. The Stock Market is where existing shareowners can sell to potential buyers. It is basically a globally connected and organized market place, where large sums of money are moved back and forth on a daily basis. It is, however, not goods that are bought and sold in this market, but instead, rights to assets are known as shares. These shares of companies are bought not from the companies themselves in these markets, but rather from an already-existing shareholder who chooses to sell the share. Similarly, when you sell your share, you do not sell it back to the company. Instead, you sell them to some other investor who wants to become a shareholder of that specific company. In the simplest of terms, the stock market demand and supply for each stock determines its market price.

There are many stock markets/exchanges around the world, but the most popular and major ones are the:

1. New York Stock Exchange (NYSE);
2. National Association of Securities Dealers Automated Quotations (NASDAQ);
3. London Stock Exchange (LSE);
4. Japan Exchange Group (JPX);
5. Shanghai Stock Exchange (SSE);
6. Korea Exchange (KRX); and
7. TMX Group (TSX). (Wikipedia, n.d.)[4]

Moving on, a financial instrument is a tradeable asset. It can also be considered a monetary contract between different parties, a contract that can be created, traded, and modified. Swing traders buy shares for a few days, and when the price has moved higher, they sell it for a profit. Let's discuss the best types of shares for a novice to trade on. These stocks are the kind that is known as 'Large-Cap' stocks. These are of companies that have a market capitalization value of greater than &10bn. These are useful because they contain various shares that change hands at any given minute, making them much easier to buy and sell.

---

[4] Wikipedia. (n.d.). List of Stock Exchanges. Retrieved from Wikipedia: https://en.wikipedia.org/wiki/List_of_stock_exchanges

The more liquid the asset, the better for swing traders. The kind of stock and share you should aim to trade as a swing trader are such that do not see excessive volatility and fluctuations in their prices. The stocks you choose should be those with steady price actions, trending slightly up or down, without large risks. The stocks should also have reliable information regarding them, and these are usually of companies that have much more at stake by not being honest. These stocks are of:

1. Microsoft Corporation;
2. Facebook; and
3. Apple.

Now you know all about swing trading, and what to do, but the question that arises is where do you look to see real-time swings? Where do you observe these changes that allow you to decide whether you should buy or sell a stock? The answer to this is Stock Charts. Let's discuss some of the basic stock charts and stock chart patterns for you as a swing trader. Of course, there are many types, but we will only discuss a few in order to help you build a foundation for learning chart patterns in proper stock charts so as to make better, more calculated trader assessments and decisions.

In today's world, there are so many different types of options for traders to pick from that it becomes quite confusing as to which instrument or chart should be consulted for the best results. The most effective type of chart and timeframe for Swing Trading is the daily time-frame. Before that, though, identify the overall trend by seeing the weekly chart to get the basic idea and direction of the price trend and movement, and then zero in on more micro trends using the daily charts, to entail more precision and accuracy in your trading decisions. The daily chart helps to dissect the trade level and refine it more easily. A single chart/time-frame is not enough for swing trading, as it required more calculated risks, which is why a multi-timeframe analysis using both weekly, then daily, charts. This basically helps you identify your entry based on a more top-down approach. Using this method, you locate the trends accurately, and trends are the primary means to a profit. This method also eliminates market noise.

Relative to Swing Trading, two types of chart patterns are used:

1. Continuation Chart Patterns; and

2. Reversal Chart Patterns. (Hayes, Introduction to Technical Analysis Price Patterns, 2020)[5]

---

[5] Hayes, A. (2020, March 27). Introduction to Technical Analysis Price Patterns. Retrieved from
Investopedia:
https://www.investopedia.com/articles/technical/112601.asp

Continuation patterns are such that help us to recognize in which direction the price is more likely to move, i.e., whether the price trend will continue or not. A stock that follows a downtrend or an uptrend is known to be a continuous chart pattern. Contrary to this, reversal chart patterns are such that signal the change of course in the trend. It indicates that an uptrend is about to reverse and that prices are going to head downwards, and vice versa.

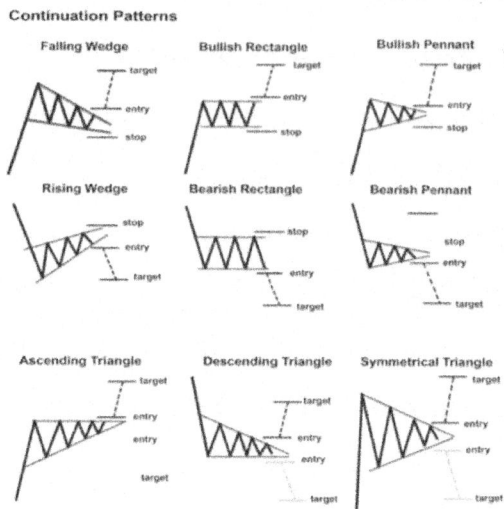

Figure 5: Continuous Chart Patterns

Source 5: How to Do Swing Trading In Stock Market - Part 3, Chart Patterns Explained; Trend Trader Karan

The different types of Continuation Patterns are:

1. **Falling Wedge:** When the stock prices start rallying upwards and then fall and rise in a downward trend when all the lower-highs and lower-lows are connected up, a downward-facing wedge-like shape is formed;

2. **Bullish Rectangle:** As the stock goes up, it formulates a sideways market, where neither lower-highs nor lower-lows exist and moves between the support and resistance levels in a sideways manner;

3. **Bullish Pennant:** quite similar to the Falling Wedge, the area of this pattern keeps getting smaller;

4. **Rising Wedge:** when an upturns stock is falling, the following consolidation forms an upward facing wedge-like shape, as seen in Figure 5;

5. **Bearish Rectangle:** the exact opposite of the Bullish Rectangle, where instead of the stock initially comes down from above;

6. **Bearish Pennant:** the opposite of the Bullish Pennant, except the price of stocks, comes down from up;

7. **Ascending Triangle:** the stock price index moves upwards and then starts fluctuation.

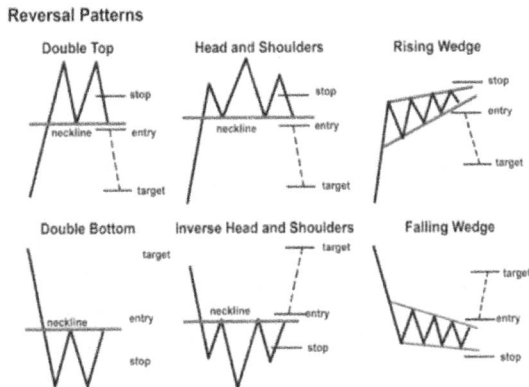

Figure 6: Reversal Chart Patterns
Source 6: How to Do Swing Trading In Stock Market - Part 3, Chart Patterns Explained; Trend Trader Karan

The higher levels remain the same throughout, but the lower turning points are higher than the preceding ones;

8. **Descending Triangle:** exactly like the Ascending Triangle, except the stock movement is reversed;

9. **Symmetrical Triangle:** with the upper turning points and lower turning points are connected to form lines, and it makes a symmetrical triangle. The entry can go in either direction;

Then there are the following types of reversal chart patterns, as shown in Figure 6. All these different chart patterns help us determine how the price trends change, helping us to identify when the stock will breakout, allowing us to make decisions of when to buy and sell the stocks in order to achieve good amounts of profit.

The most useful patterns for swing traders are the following:

1. **Sideways:** also known as the rectangles, this shows the pausing trend. The rectangle pattern allows the stock to move sideways up until the point it breaks out. As this trend is established, swing traders can recognize where they should buy or sell their stocks, depending on whether the trend is bullish or bearing. It is usually where the stock breaks out of that pattern;

2. **Stair Step:** as they continue the trend, it helps swing traders to determine the Higher-Lows in upward trends,

and Lower Highs in downtrends, making it easier to decide when to buy and sell stocks and shares;

3. **Triangles:** similar to sideways trend, again it helps swing traders to determine when the stock broke out, identifying points at which trading decisions take place;

4. **Double Top/Bottom:** if it's a bottom, then that means the price is bouncing and then goes up, and vice versa, if it's a top. The chart pattern essentially identifies a trend, and trends are a swing trader's best friend, so overall, they help to establish, at which point the trader must make a decision to buy the stock, and at which point they should sell it.

5. Fundamental Analysis:

Which are the best information sources and how to use it:
timing, volume, types of shares involved in the macroeconomic
scenario

The Fundamental Analysis is a trading discipline that focuses on a firm or corporation's financial statements to determine the fair value of a business and its stocks. With this, you end up measure the stock's intrinsic value due to the different economic and financial factors that affect the stock market and hence the stock itself. Both macroeconomic and microeconomic factors are studied, such the state of the economy and a company's efficiency respectively, however, we will focus more on the macroeconomic scenario to help you understand how economic situations are used to determine where and when a trader should buy or sell their shares and stocks, e.g., a trader might review the inventories and future projects of the diamond industry in order to assess whether supplies will increase or decrease, therefore affecting the price of diamonds, and hence the stock prices of this particular market as well. If the trader assesses that prices will go lower in the future, they will choose to sell their stock, and vice versa. This is how Fundamentals decide when to buy and sell their shares.

The Fundamental's assessment moves from a macroeconomic to a microeconomic level, trying to search for stocks that are incorrectly priced by the market. They look at the bigger picture first, then the industry in which the company operates and finally, they dig deep into a firm's financial statements, figuring out its potential for growth, revenues, Return on Equity (ROE) and general profit-making, and how much risk they are entailing. This method is known as the 'Top-Down Approach". Trading using this analysis is more commonly associated with long-term trading, such as the 'Buy and Hold' strategy, rather than active trading methods like Swing Trading, which is why we won't dwell too much on the details. However, we will clear out some basic concepts.

Let's first try to understand the meaning behind a stock's "intrinsic value." In simple words, a company's market price is disregarded, and buying and selling of stocks id dependent upon whether the stock is traded at a premium (the sum added to an ordinary price) or discount to its fair price. Fundamentalists focus more on a company's data to determine the true value of a stock, or something close to it. This form of analysis is very hypothetical, with each trader of this discipline assuming a different intrinsic value. For example, take a company 'X.'

Although X's stock might be trading at $30, one trader might determine that it is actually worth $37 after extensive research using public data, of course, while another might assess it to be worth $35. The intrinsic value of the stock is considered to be the average of all estimates, in this case, making X's stock worth $36. These estimates are important because traders want to buy the stocks trading at prices below the estimated intrinsic value, buying at a discount, in hopes that their investment will pay off when the actual trade value reaches up to the estimated one, in the long run, as it is assumed that eventually, the market will reflect the estimates made by the Fundamentals because, in the long run, they believe that under-valued stock will eventually gain its value as the market will correct itself. Though it states that in the long-run, the market will eventually get corrected, the long-term is not clearly defined, and it could vary from months to even years. The Fundament Analysis tells us nothing about the timing, and because there is so much information involved in determining the intrinsic value of a stock, it makes the process of trading quite a time consuming one for the trader. The same is the case for if the stock is overvalued. They will sell the share at the overvalued price and buy it back when the market corrects itself and goes down to the value estimated by such analysts, allowing them to make profits. The analysis done in this discipline can be both quantitative, i.e., the things that can be counted, and qualitative, which refers to the intangibles, dealing with the quality and essence of a stock. Qualitative information includes things like 'Brand-Value,' how recognized the firm is, and how effective and efficient its management is. (Segal, 2020)[6]

In the Fundamental Analysis, we focus on the economic indicators to make trading decisions, and the indicators can either be 'Leading,' 'Lagging,' or 'Coincidence.' These are labeled as so because they show change relative to the business cycle in different ways. As the names suggest, the leading indicators are ahead of the actual changes in market price, moving before the price change, due to its predictive qualities. On the contrary, lagging indicators are the opposite, bringing confirmation that the price change makes sense and that what you think you see in the price change has actually occurred. This is all theoretical, of course, and in reality, the indicators are not perfect and sometimes tend to give fake signals. This tends to occur for leading signals more often than for lagging.

Coincidence indicators change more or less around the same time as the whole economy's conditions change, helping Fundamentals to grasp at the current state of the economy. These indicators include the:

[6] Segal, T. (2020, March 16). Investopedia. Retrieved from Fundamental Analysis:
https://www.investopedia.com/terms/f/fundamentalanalysis.asp

1. **Gross Domestic Product (GDP):** the value of all final goods and services produced within the bounds of a country during a specific time period, usually a year. It provides a general idea of how productive businesses have been, and how much the economy of a country is boosting.

2. **Interest Rates:** it is essentially the rate of Bank charges for lending money. It is also the rate at which a bank pays those that save money in an account;

3. **Government Regulations and Fiscal Policies:** Fiscal policies determine how much the government will spend on the economy, or how much the government will tax its businesses.

For leading indicators, if they are right, they help you realize the price changes well in advance, but if the signal did not turn out to be true as, in reality, the market is not as predictable as we would like it to be, it could cause a lot of damage and would require really good risk management skills to cope with all the positions opened for you due to the fake signal.

For lagging indicators, the timing is an issue as you miss out on knowing changes that could have occurred and helped you profit, but because they are used as a confirmatory tool, the quality of its signals is much higher as you know for sure whether what you see if right or wrong.

Considering this discipline focuses quite a bit on the economy as a whole, many macroeconomic scenarios affect the financial stocks of particular markets as well. Generally, all those macroeconomic factors that boost businesses in your country, cause the prices and volumes of a share to increase, and vice versa. If the country's GDP growth is significantly good, or if the Fiscal Policies made by the government are favorable to businesses and their profits, the value of shares also rises. As the value of share rises, traders buy them in hopes of selling them off when they reach their peak price. If your economy as a whole is going well, the prices of stocks will also show an increasing trend. If, for instance, an economy's interest rates fall and become very low, instead of holding money and saving it in banks, traders tend to start investing in stocks in order to gain higher returns. This is because, in such periods, businesses tend to grow much more. This is because it is cheaper for businesses to take loans from banks and invest in their operations, inherently leading to a boost in their products, and hence profits.

Alternatively, if interest rates are high, businesses have lower returns, traders sell their shares, and save their money into banks. Political scenarios also tend to affect the stock market, as different governments have different agendas in mind, consequently affecting business according to their own schemata.

Sudden changes in the economy due to unpredictable situations such as a national disaster, or something we can more easily relate to, the COVID-19 Coronavirus Pandemic, also affects how the stock market moves. The current pandemic has caused economies to lock-down world-wide, gravely affecting business. This caused the stock market to 'crash,' where stock prices came to a sudden and dramatic decline across a large cross-section of the stock market, i.e., multiple different kinds of businesses and industries, too.

6. Technical Analysis:

Explication of the most important technical indicators for the swing trading: Support and Resistance levels, Moving averages, RSI, ADX, MACD, etc.

Unlike the Fundamental Analysis of stocks, the methods of Technical Analysis evaluate stocks on the basis of different charts, which determine trends, predicting future prices of the relevant stock. Where Fundamental focuses on a stock's value based on the sales and earnings of the relevant business, Technical Analysis attempts to determine stock value on its price and volume.

The trading discipline of Technical Analysis identifies different trading opportunities and evaluates investments by analyzing all the trends gathered from the price movements of a stock. It focuses on the supply and demand of the stock itself, understands how the market will change due to the market forces at play, altering the price, and volume of the stock. Just like any good or asset, even stocks' value gets altered due to its demand and supply. Without getting into too much detail, let's try to understand how this works. Shifts in the stock's demand and supply curve shift the equilibrium of the stock. The equilibrium is what determines the market price and volume. The market is altered in the following ways:

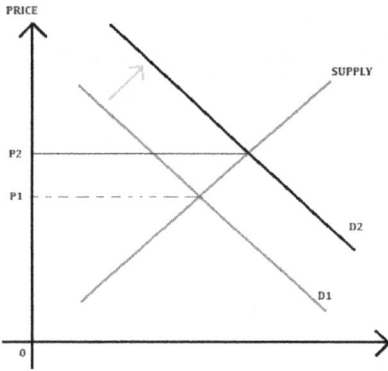

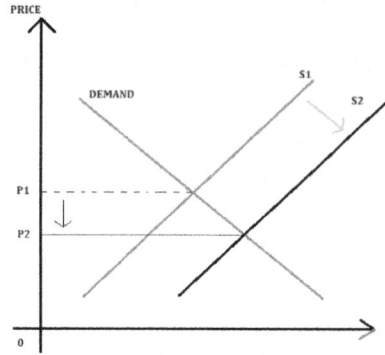

Figure 8: A shift in the Demand rightwards represents an increase in the demand for the stock. This pushes

Figure 7: A shift in the Supply curve rightwards also represents an increase in the supply. This pushes the price of the stock down, and vice versa.

Source 8: own-sourced

Source 7: own-sourced

It is a technical analysis that is used by traders to generate different trading signals from multiple different charting tools, which are short term in nature, allowing analysts to evaluate the stock market and estimating the value of the stock in a more accurate way. It is far more prevalent in stock markets where traders are focus on short-term price movements, like that of swing trading, using past trading activity and general price changes of the stock to predict its future price movements.

The pioneer for Technical Analysis was Charles Dow, founder of The Wall Street Journal. By creating the Dow-Jones Industrial Index, commonly known as 'The Dow' in 1896 with his business partner Edward Jones, he opened the door to the vast fields of Technical Analysis. The Dow Jones Industrial Index is one that tracks thirty giant, nationally recognized, and financially sound publically-owned firms that trade on the New York Stock Exchange also referred to as the NYSE, and the National Association of Securities Dealers Automated Quotations, or more commonly known as the NASDAQ. An Index is a compilation and collection of different assets, including stocks that move according to the stocks within it, and traders analyze indices in order to make trading decisions. The Dow-Jones Industrial Index is one of the oldest, most commonly observed indexes of the world, designed to proxy-represent the United States' economy in a broader manner. It is so often observed because it was composed of the shares of companies that earn quite stably throughout and will continue to earn in a stable manner consistently, such as Microsoft Corporation, Walt Disney, and multiple different industries, including that of railroads, oil, and tobacco. (Beattie, 2019)[7]

---

[7] Beattie, A. (2019, June 25). The Pioneers of Technical Analysis. Retrieved from Investopedia: https://www.investopedia.com/articles/financial-theory/10/pioneers-technical-analysis.asp

When discussing Technical Analysis, Charles Dow stated two basic assumptions that continue to create the framework for trading through this discipline, despite having evolved so much. Although now, through years of research, modern-day Technical Analysis consists of hundreds of patterns and signals, those basic assumptions still stand:

1. **The market discounts everything:** Analysts of this discipline believe that all the company earnings that fundamental analysts refer to are already represented in a company's stock, and as far as the movement of the price of a stock is concerned, it can be determined via the supply and demand changes of that relevant stock;

2. **Price moves in trends:** Regardless of the time frame, all market movements observe a trend, and erratic movement is not to be expected; and

3. **History repeats itself:** This assumption is not too different from the second one, as it states that trends are very easily predictable because they repeat themselves. (Hayes, Technical Analysis, 2020)[8]

[8] Hayes, A. (2020, March 16). Technical Analysis. Retrieved from Investopedia:
https://www.investopedia.com/terms/t/technicalanalysis.asp#how-technical-analysis-is-used

These assumptions lay true no matter what, but Technical Analysts have developed different indicators that help to identify market trends, the support and resistance areas, and even such that determine how likely it is for a trend to continue, such as:

1. Support and Resistance Levels;
2. Average Directional Index (ADX);
3. Chart Patterns (*already discussed*);
4. Oscillators; and
5. Moving Averages.

6.1 Support and Resistance Levels:

Support and Resistance Levels are one of the key concepts meant to help you while evaluating price charts as a trader. New traders tend to focus more on pivot points, but it is important to give these levels attention as well if you want to trade successfully or else you will be missing out on basic market information. In the technical analysis of the stock market, these levels are essentially predetermined price levels of stocks, at which it is assumed that the price will tend to stop and reverse itself. This is because analysts assume that at these levels, shares either become a little too expensive or a little too cheap, and they should not go beyond these levels.

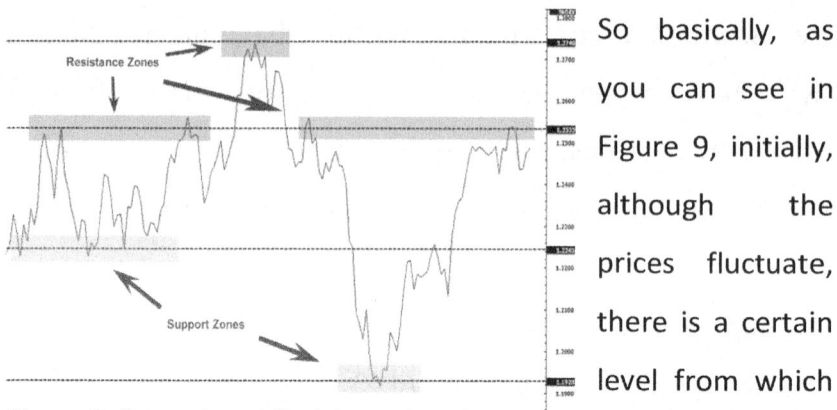

Figure 9: Support and Resistance Levels

Source 9: Forex Support and Resistance; babypips.com

So basically, as you can see in Figure 9, initially, although the prices fluctuate, there is a certain level from which they don't go above or below. These levels are determined to be the support and resistance levels. Support basically describes the price level where the downward trend of the price pauses itself, as the demand for that stock starts to increase. On the other hand, resistance is that level where the upward trend of a price reverses itself. It is the point where the market has tried to surpass before but just could not seem to go through. Certain major stock events could cause the prices to exceed beyond the resistance level, or fall below the support level as can be observed, but eventually, the stock prices come back to the trend they previously followed. These levels are so important to study as compared to other levels such as the Bollinger Bands or the Fibonacci Retracement Levels because with these, and the market is itself telling you where there have been buyers and sellers, and where exactly supply and demand exists.

Of course, it doesn't work perfectly. However, it can help a beginner out by helping them recognize obvious areas they should look at to initiate a trade. What good entry and exit points are, especially for a Swing Trader, because it helps us to see that if prices are currently approaching the resistance level, they are most likely bound to make a downturn in a few weeks and vice versa if a price is approaching a support level. They help you figure out where you want to place your trade and your 'stop-losses' in regard to the 'bid-ask spread.'

6.2 Average Directional Index (ADX):

It is an indicator used to measure the overall strength of a price trend. Developed by Wells Wilder, along with a few other indicators all together composing the 'Directional Movement System,' it essentially attempts to measure how strong the price movement of a stock is, whether that is in the positive or negative direction. Although it is technically a simple average of the values in the Directional Index, calculating the ADX yourself is quite complicated and actually unnecessary, as it is automatically done for you in whatever trading app you are using. It is quite beneficial for swing trading because it focuses on short-term periods. This is because it was invented in the late 70s when computers were not as strong as they are now, and Wilder focused on short term periods as they were easier and much more convenient to study manually.

How does it work, though? This indicator makes use of three lines; the ADX itself, a positive Directional Indicator (DI+), and a negative Directional Indicator (DI-). The ADX line itself shows the strength of the price change trend itself. The higher the line is, the stronger the trend tends to be, meaning it has continued on that path for longer periods of time. A standard of '25' was stated by Wilder, which suggested that the market was following a trend.

Points above the standard '25' suggest a strong trend was present in the market, while values below 20 show no trend to be present at that the price was very volatile, fluctuating up and down quite often. If the value of the ADX starts rising, it means a trend is beginning to form and strengthen in the market and that it will continue to do, that the market is becoming quite directional, and vice versa. This means that the value of the ADX is proportional to the trend's slope. If the slope is steeper, ADX is higher. If it is flatter or often fluctuating, the value is below 20 – 25.

The other two lines, DI+ and DI- give out signals to the trader of what trade decision they should make. If the DI- crosses below the DI+, it is a bearish signal, and vice versa. But these signals are only to be followed if the ADX line at that point is also above 25, implying that it is a trend-following market. If the ADX is below 25, you ignore the trending signals given out by the DI- and DI+. However, where it exceeds 25, the trend signals can be acted on. The higher the ADX, the better it is for you to follow the signal. Of course, it is much more complicated in actually seeing it through, and in theory, it seems much simpler, but as a beginner this all you need to not in order to prevent you from getting too confused, which I'm sure you might be quite a bit at the moment.

6.3 Oscillators–Volume & Momentum Indicators:

A leading indicator for Technical Analysis, it is used by traders when viewing price charts. The trader essentially uses these to identify at what point a stock starts to become overbought and oversold. Oscillators are very important and are used because they *potentially* give an advance warning that a change might occur in the prices of the stocks, meaning that maybe there is a 'reversal' in trends. They are constructed in such a way that their value oscillates between a neutral point. Each type of oscillator has a similar concept of being assigned values, usually between 0 and 100, but the price index represented in each oscillator is calculated through different formulas, indicating potential price changes in different ways. (Investopedia Staff, 2019)[9]

---

[9] Investopedia Staff. (2019, December 12). An Introduction to Oscillators. Retrieved from Investopedia:
https://www.investopedia.com/articles/technical/070301.asp

6.3.1 Stochastic Oscillator:

The Stochastic Oscillator is a momentum oscillator, which looks at the momentum of the price, i.e., the rate at which the price changes. Developed by Dr. George Lane, a technical analyst, in the 1950s, this technical indicator lets the trader know what stock has been over-bought and over-sold, comparing current prices to those of the past, not just by comparing older prices but by considering the highest and lowest price ever recorded across the period selected by the trader. This form of comparison is known as 'Lookback,' quite literally because you are looking back at older prices.

The values of this indicator are bounded between 0 and 100, and it generally appears below the normal price chart, as shown in Figure 10.

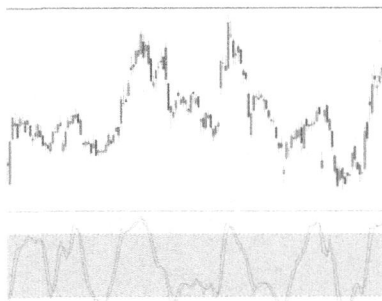

Figure 10: Stochastic Oscillator

Source 10: Stochastic Oscillator Definition; Investopedia

It consists of two lines, one known as '%K,' which represents current prices relative to the time period being observed, and the other one known as '%D,' which is the average price. Both these percentages are calculated by formulas, which you need not get into as a beginner. Both these lines run paths similar to each other's, following the same trends in general, and they occasionally intersect as well. It also shows two lines, within which stocks seem to be fine, represented by the shaded region in Figure 10. The upper bound, at '80', indicates that stocks at prices above it has been overbought, while the lower bound at '20' represents stocks with prices below this bound have been oversold. These 'overbought' and 'oversold' lines are representors of potential reversals in price as beyond these points, and the market cannot sustain itself.

When your oscillator exceeds the line represents 'overbought stocks,' it's a warning sign to not buy more stocks and that the market will eventually fall, and when it starts dipping back down, that's your sign to sell your stocks.

Similarly, when the oscillator surpasses the 'oversold' line, it warns you that your price levels are about to reach a bottom, and once it starts going back up, it indicates that you should start buying your stocks again.

The cross overs of '%K' and '%D' are trading signals as well. For example, if %K was to crossover below %D, then you would sell your stocks, as the current price is moving below the average, and vice versa. Moreover, if you notice that your oscillator is not following the trend of the actual price chart at a certain point, i.e., initially both the price chart and oscillator had a decreasing trend, but after a point, the oscillator starts to rise, it indicates a *potential* reversal in prices, a possibility of a turning point. This is known as 'Divergence,' i.e., there is a disagreement between the actual price change as compared to the one predicted by the indicator. 'Potential' was specifically highlighted, however, because it isn't important for a divergence to occur at every turning point.

6.3.2 Relative Strength Index (RSI):

The Relative Strength Index is another momentum oscillator. First talked about and invented in his book "New Concepts in Trading Systems" by J. Welles Wilder in the 1970s, the RSI, and just like any other oscillator, it assigns the stocks being observed values between 0 and 100. Using these values, the index is compared with other factors, such as the overbought, prices above the value of '70' and oversold, prices below '30', values, similar to the Stochastic Oscillator. The difference is, though, that this index is charted on a daily time frame to recognize whether or not it is smart to make short-term stock purchases. In short, it measures the magnitude of recent price changes. However, the signals it gives do tend to be more reliable when looking at the long-term trend. It tends to give false alarms, as most leading indicators do, and considering it displays momentum of price change, it is possible for the price of the stock to remain above overbought or below oversold if the stock has a significant amount of momentum in either direction. It should be used in markets that fluctuate much more often.

6.3.3 Rate of Change Indicator (ROC):

Also, being a momentum oscillator, the Rate of Change Indicator focuses on the current prices but relative to prices an 'n' number of periods ago. The older price is known as the 'lookback' price. Unlike the stochastic and RSI indicator, the Rate of Change Indicator oscillates around 0 and not between values of 0 and 100. This is what this oscillator shows us: when the current price is greater than that of the lookback, you get positive values, and the index is above the 'zero-line,' that the market price is stronger than it had been, and when it is lower, you get negative values, moving the index below the line indicating that the market price is weaker than it had been, which is a shift in the momentum. This means that when they are equal, you get a value of zero. When the index swings from positive to negative across the zero line, it is considered a bearish signal, implying that prices might lower, and vice versa, indicating a bullish signal that prices are likely to rise.

6.4 Moving Averages:

A technical analysis indicator, lagging in nature, helps to smooth out price action in short-term price fluctuations by filtering out noise and 'randomness.' They lag behind the current price because they make use of older prices, which is why they are much better for short-term trading like swing trading. After all, the lag is smaller when smaller periods are taken into account. A 300-day Moving Average will have a much higher lag as compared to a 50-day Moving Average. All in all, it is the average of the price changes. It is based on past prices, used to identify the general trend direction. Amongst many, there are two types of Moving Averages as explained below:

1. *Simple Moving Average (SMA):* It is calculated by taking the arithmetic mean of prices (sum of prices/the number of prices). It helps in determining whether or not the stock will continue on its trend, whether that is bull or bear, by smoothing out the volatility, making it much easier to view the trend. If it points up, the price of the stock is increasing, and if it points down, the price of the stock is decreasing;

2. *Exponential Moving Average (EMA):* Calculates a more weighted average as it focuses more on recent prices, making it respond more quickly to price changes of the

stock. Due to this quick response attribute, most traders prefer it over the Simple Moving Average.

The rising Moving Average indicates an uptrend and vice versa. The reason they are liked by many traders is that they are much more customizable as compared to other indicators, by choosing the amount of time period you want to observe and study, though preference is always given to short time periods though because in such cases this indicator is more sensitive, hence gives confirmation of price changes quicker.

Although useful on its own, it also forms the basis for the **Moving Average Convergence Divergence (MACD)**, a trend-following momentum indicator which essentially indicates the relationship between two moving averages of a stock's price. Two moving averages of different time periods are essentially formulated, short-term and long-term, and then the difference between the two is calculated. The most common Moving Averages for this indicator are a 26-day EMA and a 12-day EMA.

If the long term is above that of the short term, the difference gives a positive result (the line will oscillate above the center/zero lines) which indicates upward momentum, telling the trader to buy, and vice versa, i.e., if the difference is negative, the trend is downwards (the line will oscillate below the centerline), telling the trader to sell. (Hayes, Moving Averages (MA), 2020)[10]

---

[10] Hayes, A. (2020, April 22). Moving Averages (MA). Retrieved from Investopedia:
https://www.investopedia.com/terms/m/movingaverage.asp

In a way, the **Bollinger Band®**, invented and copyrighted by John Bollinger, is also an off-spring of the Moving Averages. These are essentially volatility bands placed two standard deviations above and below a 20-day simple moving average

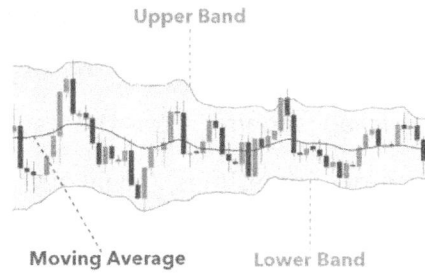

Figure 11: Bollinger Bands

Source 11: How to Use Bollinger Bands® in Forex Trading; dailyfx.com

of the stock's price. However, the time period can always be adjusted according to the traders' wants. Since the volatility is dependent upon the standard deviation between the prices, as volatility increases, the band widens, and as it decreases, the bands become narrower, as shown in Figure 11. This is because as volatility changes, so does the Standard Deviation. There is no need for you to learn how to calculate these Bands as most software does it for you automatically, but it is important to know what these bands mean. When the bands come closer together towards the moving average, known as a 'squeeze,' it means that prices are less volatile and that prices will fluctuate more in the future, bringing about new trading opportunities.

The wider the upper and lower band means that price volatility is less likely, and it brings about opportunities to exit a trade. This is all shown 'after the fact,' though, as it is a lagging indicator. Sometimes, 'breakouts' occur, which refers to when the actual prices go beyond the bands. It is important to understand that these are not trading signals, but just mere coincidences that do not inform you of much. Do not assume these to be indicators of when to buy or sell.

Technical Analysis is often brushed off by traders because they believe the study of charts and price trends is too superficial, but once mastered, it can give you sizeable profits. Although it is quite profitable for short-term trading such as swing trading, it existed long before computers were common, and many pioneers of technical analysis were long-term traders. Many traders owe their success to this discipline of trading, so even you can become an advanced trader with time by studying stock charts and price trends of a market.

Predicting trends in the stock market is an extremely complicated process, but using these indicators, you can help yourself have better odds. As a novice, you should try to get the hang of these indicators in 'practice' mode of whichever app you use, so as to better understand them because it is not as quick and easy as some might have you believe.

Even that which has been explained to you in this book is only a brief description of each indicator, and there is a lot more science that you need to understand in order to use these indicators effectively. Although technical analysis software makes it easier to see different trends, how to analyze and interpret them is your job, and that only comes with experience.

7. Swing Trading Rules and Strategies:

Consider swing trading as a business; Setup a business plan;
Manage the Risk and the Revenue Ratio;

Warren Buffett, one of the world's best investors and business tycoons, said that *"Only buy something that you'd be perfectly happy to hold if the market shut down for 10 years."* That means, when investing, whether you aim to become an active trader or a passive one, it is important to buy stocks that are also better for long-term investment, in case the market ever goes south.

It is pertinent to buy safe stocks, such as those whose price changes are shown in 'The Dow.' If you do business out of your Swing Trading, make sure that more than 80% of the stocks you invest in are safe stocks, ones you know will never reach 0 or close to 0, such as the stocks of Microsoft Corporation or Coca-Cola. These firms increase their dividends on an annual basis, so their stocks have risen quite steadily over the past couple of years. Keep in mind, though, that you shouldn't invest all your money in a single stock, but should invest some money in one kind of stock, another in a different kind, and so on. This is because in case one stock ended up plummeting, you still had the other investments to help you make good returns.

You can also invest in Exchange-Traded Funds (ETF), which sort of a collection of assets like stocks and bonds of a specific market like the Tech Industry. However, that is a discussion for another time. It is also important to buy when everyone else is selling. This is because when a lot of people start selling their stocks, it is because they predict the market to get bad very soon and is reaching a point of the recession. People start selling because they do not want to lose any more money, and you can use this to your advantage. You can use recessions to earn a lot of money because, after a recession, the stock prices can only go up. At the same time, however, if the value of the stock you have bought suddenly goes down, and remains down for large periods whether that is weeks, months or even years, do not become scared and do not sell your stock, because it is very likely that the stock will go back up. The only time you should sell your stocks is when you know that the supply of a stock is about to rise, devaluing it, or that an economy is about to undergo a serious recession, but these decisions have to be made prior to the plummet of stick prices. During a fall, only sell when you absolutely feel it to be necessary. Similarly, only sell when everyone is buying. For a successful business in trading, another advice would be to not invest less than $500 at a time. Most people trade with the help of professional brokers or via the banks, so every time you buy a share, there is a fee that you have to pay, which varies depending on whether you're buying a domestic or foreign stock. Essentially, if you invest less, the fee ends up being more than the return you get on your trade, so you don't really make any money. Percentage returns on stocks are usually low, ranging from 5% - 10%. If you invest $200 via the online broker 'Fidelity,' the fee is currently $32.95. A 10% return on your trade would mean you made $20, which is less than the fee. On the other hand, if you invest $700, the return you would get $70, leaving you with $37.05. Large investments in your stocks lead to greater payoffs, especially in Swing Trading, where general profit levels are higher.

As Swing Trading becomes more and more common, due to the fact that it produces predictable price actions, it is easy to set up a business in this form of trading. To make trading into a business, you must actually think of it as a business also. Rather than look at trading as some side project, focus on it as though you were the CEO of your own trade business. Your mindset alone will determine whether trading will cost you money or make it.

After doing enough research, formulate your business plan in a comprehensive manner. As a Swing Trader, you've already answered the first question for your plan: the kind of trader you want to be.

But a plan includes many more things, such as which system of risk management and which tools you will opt for and utilize. Lastly, decide the kind of setups you will focus on. The business plan will make your trading more focused, brushing away a lot of different factors that complicate trading. The simpler trading is for you, the better. (Comit, 2018)[11]

Risk Management Systems are strategies to minimize costs and maximize returns. Most successful traders use the Stock Market Risk Management Strategies to do so. These strategies focus on what the best entry and exit points are, where you will get the greatest returns. These strategies include the 'Stop-Loss and Take-Profit,' 'Diversify and Hedge,' and 'The Bottom Line,' discussed in the next segment of this book. A Swing Trader also makes use of Risk and Revenue Ratios, which assess a firm's revenue with the risk level due to the firm's debt. Before investing in a company, investors use these ratios to assess whether or not the firm can manage its outstanding debt, a major determinant of its stock's value. The prospective reward that can be earned by a trader is marked by the Risk to Reward Ratio.

---

[11] Comit. (2018, August 7). Learn How to Make a Trading Plan. Retrieved from Vantage Point Trading:
https://vantagepointtrading.com/learn-how-to-make-a-trading-plan/

It is usually already calculated in the Technical Analysis software being used by the trader. A good ratio is < 1, and vice versa. (Kuepper, 2019)[12]

For Swing Trading, there are different platforms, tools, and brokers that you can make use of to make trades. Platforms include different Technical Analysis Software or Web-Based Technical Chart Platforms. Both of these are beneficial for Swing Trading. Technical Software helps you to customize your indicators to your specific needs, and it is pre-screen ready, so you can pick out trades directly from it. The Web-Based Technical Chart Platforms have drawbacks, but it is still okay to use them. However, it would be better in the long-run for you to invest your money in good software such as Ninjatrader and Amibroker. This is because the software has hundreds of different tools that you can use, which were previously discussed, such as the RSI, ROC, and the Moving Averages.

Brokers are more complicated, and you should be very careful with the kind you choose. A Broker will buy or sell assets for you or give you advice on how you should buy and sell your assets, depending on the kind of service you hire them for.

---

[12] Kuepper, J. (2019, August 19). Risk Management Techniques for Active Traders. Retrieved from
Investopedia: https://www.investopedia.com/articles/trading/09/risk-management.asp

Specifically, in regard to Swing Trading, you should choose a Discount Broker. This is because profit margins are often low, and so you don't want that all your profits are spent on fee costs. The problem with this is that during Event heavy days, low-cost brokers face a lot of problems, and their system freezes, preventing orders from going through, so this is something you should be wary of. Before choosing a specific broker, research upon it and try to figure out via different forums what different traders' experiences were like and how they have reviewed it. If their system freezes, how did they deal with it, and did they cater to the needs of their customers? Do they have good customer service? All these questions are very important and should be taken into account and clarified before choosing your Broker.

Once you make all your decisions and formulate a business plan, stick to the game plan you have chosen, so that it's simpler for you to analyze the changes and trends of stock prices because you will slowly become more and more familiar with the different aspects you have selected. Initially, practice your stock trading on simulations to get a grip on the plan, before applying it into the real world stock market. In short, test your plan out.

8. The Entry and the Exit:

How to enter on a position: objective, timing, stop loss, take profit

How to exit from a position: optimizing the profit, minimizing the losses

It has previously already been briefly discussed on when to enter and exit on a position, i.e., buy and sell your stocks, respectively. In this segment, we will take some real-life examples to help you better understand when to do what. But before that, let us discuss a few risk management techniques implemented by stock traders such as the 'Stop-Loss and Take-Profit', and 'Diversify and Hedge.'

The two points, Stop-Loss (S/L) and Take-Profit (T/P), are key ways allowing traders to plan ahead. They both are computer-based trading tools carried out by quite a sum of brokers, in which each point is a specified price level. Traders only want to execute the trade, whether it is to sell their stock or buy it if these price levels are reached.

As the names suggest, Stop-Loss is meant to limit the loss of an investor. It is a trade order placed to the trader's brokerage, and the trade is executed once the stock price falls to the stop price. Imagine that you invested in a company's share at $475 per share, and now the shares are rising, having reached a price of $540 per share.

Since the trend of the price is upwards, you want to continue to hold the stock. The issue with this is that it puts a risk on your unrealized gains (gains you haven't received yet because you haven't sold the stock). You would choose a price level, e.g., in this case, $490, after reviewing the data of the relevant firm, and decide and make a deal with your broker that if the shares were to fall below $490, you would want to sell out of your position. This helps to monitor the price for you, without you having to watch the market every other day. Take-Profit works in a similar manner. These limit orders are closed once a specified profit level is reached. Both these techniques are helpful because the trader doesn't have to manually execute trades, constantly second-guessing themselves. The Take-Profit technique is best for Swing Traders due to its short-term nature. As soon as the planned profit target is achieved, traders get out of the trade, not risking experiencing a downturn of the market. The only issue with this is that the market could continue to rise beyond these points, maybe giving you higher returns, but upon reaching it, the position is closed as the stock is sold at the decided profit level.

As previously discussed, it is vital to not invest all of your money in a single type of stock. This is known as the 'Diversify and Hedge' strategy. Diversify your investments by buying/selling stocks of different industries and companies, whether that is domestic or foreign. Hedging is a sort of an insurance policy, used by traders to control the exposure to risk by taking an offsetting position in a different but related security. The only problem with Hedging is that by reducing risks, it also reduces potential gains in case the stock you hedge against does well and booms.

Moving on, let us try to understand how you would enter or exit a market using a real-life example.

Look at BANKNIFTY Chart below. I will use this to explain how and at what points you should enter and exit from your positions.

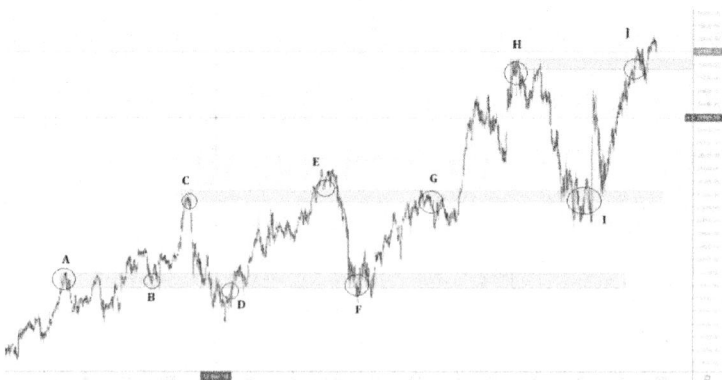

Figure 12: BANKNIFTY Price Index Chart
Source 12: How To Do Swing Trading In Stock Market - Part 1; Trend Trader Karan – youtube.com

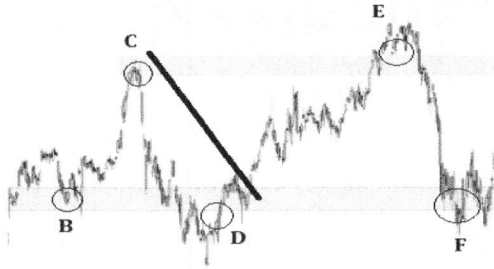

Figure 13: BANKNIFTY Price Index
Source 13: How To Do Swing Trading In Stock Market - Part 1;
Trend Trader Karan- youtube.com

Initially, the price kept rising until it reached point 'A.' In this area, the price was rejected by the market and took a turnover and went down. After some fluctuations, the price broke out through the resistance level, formulating a new resistance level at point 'C.' The old resistance level became a support for the price movement, which is further proven when the price fall is rejected at point 'D,' and it starts to rise again. It isn't necessary that the price levels will oscillate between the support and resistance levels, they do tend to break out, but these trends help us to determine when to enter on a position and when to exit it.

Refer to Figure 13. From point 'C' to 'D', you make your short-term trend line, Around point D, you enter on a position, because the support level implies that the price will go up because that is the usual trend it follows. As the price levels go up, you hold onto your position until it reaches the resistance levels. You know that at the point 'E', the price level increase will be rejected, and they will start to fall back down, so at this point, you ideally exit your position by selling your stock. This would give you a large percentage rate of return, allowing you to make large sums of profits the more shares you have. The greater money you risk, the higher returns you get.

This is how you basically enter on a position and hold it till you decide it is best to exit the position, keeping in mind all the risk preventing strategies also discussed above.

9. Trading Psychology and Discipline

Numerous abilities are required for exchanging effectively in the money related markets. They incorporate the capacities to assess an organization's essentials and to decide the heading of a stock's pattern. Be that as it may, neither of these specialized abilities is as significant as the dealer's outlook.

Containing feeling, thinking rapidly, and practicing discipline are parts of what we may call exchanging brain research. There are two fundamental feelings to comprehend and monitor: dread and avarice.

Transferring the money related markets is an exceptionally functional movement. To get fruitful as a dealer, you need excellent comprehension of the budgetary demands, and how they work, you need a decent understanding of the organizations you exchange, and you need the specialized ability to break down market patterns, just as an incredible comprehension of the elements that move the market.

In any case, even with all these specialized abilities, it is difficult to turn into a capable broker on the off chance that you need one essential quality – the exchanging brain research. The exchanging brain research is necessarily the correct attitude and the capacity to think and react quickly, stay restrained, and practice command over your feelings in any event, when the market is conflicting with your desires.

Consider these situations:

A dealer is watching the business sectors trusting that the exact second will get included. Frequently, our dealer fears losing cash, so it is reasonable that he is acting a piece mindfully. He sits tight for a superior helpline before getting into an exchange, yet then he misses the section, and the business sectors take off without him. Nothing to stress over, however. He chooses to hold up a piece and catch the next wave, but since he fears facing challenges, he misses the following section too. This happens on various occasions.

While this is occurring, our broker is conversing with other dealer companions and cooperating with different merchants in different online gatherings and gatherings. The multiple brokers are discussing the incredible benefits they have made over the most recent few weeks, yet our merchant has not entered a solitary exchange. The dread of facing challenges begins transforming into covetousness. He starts feeling like he is passing up all the benefits others are making, and he begins feeling restless and sort of disappointed, regardless of whether he has not lost any cash. To abstain from keeping passing up a great opportunity while others are bringing in stock, our broker chooses to take a hazard next time.

Driven by insatiability, he tosses all alert to the breeze and hops onto what is by all accounts a promising pattern without directing due industriousness. Sadly, the business sectors pivot.

Previously, he wasn't losing any cash, yet now he is. As opposed to assuming a misfortune, he chooses to clutch the exchange of the expectation that the business sectors will pivot and permit him to recover the cash he has recently lost. Tragically, the pattern proceeds, and he loses more money. The dissatisfaction of losing transforms into outrage, and he begins considering how to recover all his cash. Expecting that the business sectors can't go any lower, he chooses to place more money into the exchange now with the goal that he can counterbalance his misfortunes and make a clean benefit because clearly, the kit is impossible the costs will continue falling.

Be that as it may, as any active merchant knows, the business sectors are not ordinary, so the descending pattern proceeds and our broker winds up losing all his cash. Contingent upon how much money he lost, our dealer may even get into despair. The above is an extraordinary delineation of how permitting feelings to go out of control can cause you to lose your better judgment and affect your prosperity as a dealer.

Each competent dealer realizes that the business sectors are continually trying brokers, and anybody without the privilege of mental attitude and the capacity to control his feelings will make some hard memories settling on the correct choices. The following are a few other exchanging issues that are generally brought about by a dealer's brain research.

Not assuming misfortune: The commonplace explanation for this is typical that the dealer fears disappointment, which puts his self-image in question. Leaving exchanges too soon: This usually is brought about by the broker's requirement for moment delight. The merchant is on edge and frightful that the position may switch, so he chooses to close the situation to assuage the tension. Averaging down: This alludes to circumstances where the broker is reluctant to concede that their exchange isn't right. Trusting that the transfer will return, the dealer includes the losing position. This is additionally brought about by the dealer's sense of self.

Wishing and trusting: This shows itself when merchants execute exchanges dependent on their expectations and wishes, as opposed to following the market circumstance. Enthusiastic exchanging: This happens when a dealer gets dependent on exchanging, in comparative design, to how card sharks get dependent on betting.

Feeling strong: After a progression of winning exchanges, a few dealers may feel like they are invulnerable and in charge of the business sectors.

This regularly prompts dangerous trades. Re-thinking your signs: This is usually brought about by the dread of disappointment and the terror of being off-base. Dealers who second theory their symptoms generally make some hard memories tolerating that misfortune is an individual piece of exchanging. Exchanging a huge position size: This is regularly brought about by the frustration that exchange can just end up being productive, only as a reduced hazard to the executives.

Over the top exchanging: This is brought about by covetousness, and a need to conquer the market. It can likewise be brought about by outrage when a dealer is attempting to compensate for past misfortunes. Being hesitant to enter positions: This is generally brought about by dread of disappointment, chance averseness, the requirement for control dread of being disparaged, or absence of an exchanging framework. There is a lot all the more exchanging issues that are brought about by the broker's brain research, yet these are by a wide margin the most well-known. While experiencing the above circumstances, you may have seen that the dominant part of brain research-related issues are typically brought about by three feelings – dread, eagerness, and outrage.

These three feelings assume an extremely exceptional job in a trader's brain science, and any fruitful merchant must figure out how to place them under tight restraints. (Curtis, 2020)[13]

---

[13] Curtis, G. (2020, April 4). The Importance of Trading Psychology. Retrieved from Investopedia: https://www.investopedia.com/articles/trading/02/110502.asp

9.1 The Different Emotion's experienced by a Trader:

9.1.1 Fear:

Fear is a characteristic human response to anything saw as a risk – on account of the exchange, and the danger is the chance of losing cash. The bigger the potential misfortune, the higher the measure of dread experienced. Dread during exchanging shows itself in various manners. The most well-known sign of fear is, in effect, too hesitant to even think about getting included. Like our dealer from the model up over, your dread of losing cash makes you excessively mindful, and thus, you wind up missing every one of your entrances. While being wary is a significant characteristic, being too aware to the degree of missing every one of your entries transforms into a hindrance, since you won't bring in any cash in the market except if you get into exchanges. In some cases, the dread may come when you have just entered a position. Some breaking news about the stock you are exchanging, or the general market may cause a transitory development in the market.

In such circumstances, a frightful merchant may be constrained to leave the situation before their preplanned exit to abstain from losing cash. While such a dread driven leave will assist you with maintaining a strategic distance from inevitable misfortune, it additionally keeps you from making gains once the market recuperates from the impermanent unpredictability brought about by the news. On the other hand, somebody may leave a position early because they fear to hold a situation for over a day.

9.1.2 Greed:

Greed is something contrary to fear.

Though dread shields you from exchanging or makes you exit out of positions early because to dodge misfortune, avarice drives you into dangerous exchanges. It makes you hold opinions for longer than you intended to with the desire to make enormous additions. Voracity is regularly brought about by the dread of passing up a great opportunity (FOMO). This generally occurs in one of two different ways. The first is the place you see others making immense gains in the market while you haven't made any massive additions.

All together not to pass up the increase's others are making; you desert your exchanging technique and enter exchanges at an inappropriate time. A pattern proceeds past your arranged take benefit levels, and as opposed to taking benefit, you dispose of your system and keep holding the position since you fear to leave more benefits on the table. Shockingly, if the business sectors converse, all the increases you had made can without much of a stretch get cleared out very quickly.

As a broker, beating avarice can be very testing, since it is regularly brought about by the drive to improve or make somewhat more significant additions. Be that as it may, there are two principle ways to deal with defeating insatiability. The first is to quit worrying about what your companions and different merchants are doing or the significant increases they are making. As a broker, all your emphasis ought to be on your exchanges and your outcomes. You ought to be driven by the longing to improve your exchanging technique, as opposed to the craving to make what others are making.

9.1.3 Anger:

This feeling reappears when you have been not able to control the other two emotions, bringing about your exchanges conflicting with your desires. You begin feeling baffled. Outrage is quite often focused on a person or thing – for this situation, and anger is typically focused on the market. In an offer to settle the score with the market, irate dealers will frequently wind up taking part in retribution exchanging.

For example, let us expect that a merchant is in a triumphant exchange that has just arrived at the dealer's arranged take benefit point. In any case, because of failure to control his insatiability, rather than taking benefit, the dealer chooses to keep holding the exchange the expectations of hitting a grand slam. Sadly, the market turns around, and every one of his benefits is cleared out. Now, he has returned to where he began. While the increases he had at first made have been cleared out, he, despite everything, hasn't made any misfortune.

The idea of the considerable number of improvements he had and neglected to take, in any case, drives him mad and disappointed. Rather than shutting the exchange now, he may choose to trust that the market will turn around again so he can at any rate close with a slight benefit. Lamentably, this doesn't occur, and his exchange currently goes into misfortune.

A few dealers may get off now, while others may even average down in the desire for recovering their disasters, which will no doubt lead to much more noteworthy troubles.

The way to forestalling outrage is to adhere to your arrangement. In addition to the fact that this gives you authority over the other two feelings that lead to insult when they turn wild, it likewise keeps you from committing an error, for example, averaging down.

9.2 Price Action and Psychology Discipline:

Value activity portrays the qualities of security's value developments. This development is regularly examined concerning value changes in the ongoing past. In straightforward terms, value activity is an exchanging strategy that permits a dealer to peruse the market and settle on ideal exchanging choices dependent on the ongoing and real value developments, as opposed to depending exclusively on specialized pointers.

Since it overlooks the essential investigation factors and concentrates more on later and past value development, the value activity exchanging methodology is reliant on specialized examination devices. (Seth, 2019)[14]

Figure 14: Rising Wedge Uptrend Pattern
Source 14: Own Sourced

---

[14] Curtis, G. (2020, April 4). The Importance of Trading Psychology. Retrieved from Investopedia:
https://www.investopedia.com/articles/trading/02/110502.asp

9.2.1 Instruments Used for Price Action Trading:

Since value activity exchanging identifies with late verifiable information and past value developments, all specialized investigation instruments like diagrams, pattern lines, value groups, high and low swings, specialized degrees (of help, obstruction, and solidification), and so forth are considered according to the merchant's decision and technique fit.

The instruments and examples saw by the dealer can be straightforward value bars, value groups, break-outs, pattern lines, or complex blends, including candles, instability, channels, and so on.

Mental and conduct understandings and ensuing activities, as chosen by the broker, likewise make up a significant part of value activity exchanges. E.g., regardless of what occurs, if a stock floating at 580 crosses the by and by a set mental degree of 600, at that point, the merchant may accept a further upward move to take a long position. Different merchants may have a contrary view – when 600 is hit, the person in question agrees with a value inversion and subsequently makes a short position.

No two merchants will decipher a specific value activity similarly, as each will have their translation, characterized rules, and distinctive conduct comprehension of it. Then again, a specialized examination situation (like 15 DMA traverse 50 DMA) will yield comparative conduct and activity (long position) from different merchants.

Fundamentally, value activity exchanging is an orderly exchanging practice, supported by specialized investigation instruments and late value history, where merchants are allowed to take their own choices inside an offered situation to take exchanging positions, according to their emotional, social and mental state.

9.2.2 Who Uses Price Action Trading?

Since value activity exchanging is a way to deal with value expectations and hypothesis, retail merchants, examiners, arbitrageurs utilize it, and in any event, transferring firms who use brokers. It very well may be used on a broad scope of protection, including values, bonds, forex, products, subordinates, and so on.

6.2.3 Beyond the Price Pattern:

Changes in cost happen because of purchasing and selling pressure. As purchasing pressure (for example, request) surpasses the strength of sale (for example, supply), the value climbs. What's more, as selling pressure (for example, supply) exceeds purchasing pressure (for example, request), the value descends. As a broker, you endeavor to "see" where the value design is going and place your exchanges as needs are. If you somehow managed to confirm that a specific example is in a downtrend, you would generally see a likelihood that the case would proceed with descending (except if you verify that the downtrend is concluding). Also, comparatively, if you establish that a value design is in an upturn or exchanging range, you expect that the example will proceed with that path until you see some sign that shows in any case. (PSG Staff)[15]

---

[15] PSG Staff. (n.d.). Market Psychology Methods and Discipline of Trading Success. Retrieved from PSG:
https://www.psg.co.za/support/tutorials/market-psychology-method

It would consequently be valuable for you to have the option to decide the hidden pattern of given value design. Now in an examination, numerous dealers are bewildered by issues of blended or ill-advised viewpoints and the inclusion of feelings. For example, taking a gander at a value design for the most recent hour may show an unmistakable upturn, yet taking a gander at the most recent eight hours may demonstrate that the most recent hour's development was an inconsequential amendment and that the original pattern of the value design is a downtrend. The key to deciding the basic model of any value design is to look past the example. Each value design structures as a result of progress, and change is an aftereffect of purchasing and selling pressure. This weight is a consequence of the choice's financial specialists (basically institutional speculators), and brokers make as far as what they foresee. Eventually, a given value design is the aftereffect of the activities of speculators and dealers. These activities depend on investigations and assessments of how the value example will shape. What's more, here, obviously, there is, to some degree, a cycle since speculators and dealers are developing sentiments about what different financial specialists and merchants think and will do.

9.3 Discovering 'Flow':

In exchanging and sports, it is known as being "in the zone." Psychologist Mihaly Csikszentmihalyi calls top encounters "stream." People experience "stream" when they invest energy in pleasant exercises, exercises they find charming for the wellbeing of their own. During a stream understanding, one performs well beyond desires. The stream is a Zen feeling. It is like reflection or extreme fixation. It is a sense of self-less state when every one of your activities become programmed. You may see that on the off chance that one exchanges a condition of stream, the person in question will achieve an elevated level of exchanging execution.

The stream was all the more as often as possible experienced in work exercises when one is attempting to take care of testing issues, and in interests and home exercises, for example, cooking, sewing, photography, or singing. Sports were likewise helpful for encountering stream. What do these exercises share practically speaking? To start with, they require an engaged and requested condition of awareness. One must be centered on the assignment and not permit any interruptions to separation cognizance. Rock climbers are probably going to encounter this kind of focused consideration.

A stone climber must give all regard for climbing and not be occupied by considering how high one is climbing or whether one will fall. Second, these exercises include an equivalent measure of aptitude and challenge. On the off chance that a test is too incredible contrasted with one's ability, it causes stress, nervousness, and separation of cognizance. Then again, if the undertaking is excessively simple, it is seen as exhausting.

By what means can exchange be changed into a stream understanding? Ensure that you set up conditions to make exchanging fun and agreeable. Transferring inevitably is a test, yet a few brokers are overpowered, and this isn't helpful for a stream. The stunt is finding a fair compromise between exchanging methodologies that challenge your aptitudes, however, don't surpass them. On the off chance that one attempts to put on massive exchanges or use procedures and techniques that are past one's capacity, for instance, stream won't be experienced. At the point when this occurs, merchants feel stress and uneasiness. They can't concentrate on checking their exchanges. So, if you need to encounter stream and perform at your most high potential, the key is to define suitable objectives. Deal with your hazard. Build up an all-around characterized exchanging plan dependent on your present comprehension of the business sectors.

Try not to cause transferring more mind-boggling than you can see directly here and at this moment. Try not to exchange past your capacities. As you exchange as per your present abilities and gain limited quantities of ground, you will encounter exchanging as charming. You will have the option to concentrate on exchanging the business sectors with an elevated level of centered consideration, in a similar perspective that a competitor encounters when playing sports, an artist feels while moving, or a craftsman encounters while making artistry. Before long, your abilities will grow significantly more, and you can confront much all the more testing exchanging objectives. With more remarkable and more prominent experience, you will discover exchanging progressively charming, experience more prominent degrees of stream, and keep on sharpening your exchanging abilities. A stream is an ideal state for merchants. It merits figuring out how you can encounter more stream while exchanging.

9.4 Inclinations to Follow:

One of the most disturbing things for a broker to learn is when to control their desires, and when to give them free rein. The explanation is that the vast majority of your urges originate from gut feel, and have little to do with the chilly, ascertaining thinking that shapes the reason for most great exchanging choices. However, from time to time, you get an urge that you should follow, because it speaks to the entirety of all that you have found out about exchanging effectively. It offers an edge on getting a significant addition that most different dealers have not yet observed. Here are a few rules to assist you with segregating between desires to overlook, and inclinations to follow:

If it bodes well: Emotional desires will, in general, go against reason. They resemble wagering R1 000 on a single turn of a roulette wheel where they positively may come up champs. However, risks are they would not. However, different desires rise out of progressively standard mental procedures that you may not know about, yet which are by and by legitimate. At the point when you look at your inclinations in more detail, you locate that some of them precisely consider the smallest subtleties of what you know, and fit in with your most profound comprehension of how the market works.

To put it, while every one of your inclinations may contain an uncommon sort of inferential jump, some include thinking in which you can't punch any gaps. (Rolf)[16]

On the off chance that it follows your strategy: The central part of passionate urges come out of fantasy land and would be a significant flight for you to follow up on. However, a couple of your desires fit inside your exchanging technique. This merit considering, because they offer the chance to take advantage of an alternate degree of information and mindfulness without bargaining the components of exchanging -, for example, consistency and excellent conditions that are basic for progress.

On the off chance that it is generally safe: Many passionate desires are of the "Damn the Torpedoes" assortment - on the off chance that they turn out inadequately, the punishment can be very severe. These are the sort of urges you will do well to stand up to. Be that as it may, different inclinations completely fuse your built-up chance administration and cash the executive's procedures. Since there is no additional drawback on the off chance that one of these urges ends up being incorrect, they might merit testing.

---

[16] Rolf. (n.d.). How To Create A Trading Routine That Allows You To Reach Your Full Potential As A Trader.
Retrieved from EdgeWonk: https://edgewonk.com/how-to-create-a-trading-routine-that-allows-
you-to-reach-your-full-potential-as-a-trader/

9.5 Changing Your Personality to Suit Your Trading Lifestyle:

Numerous fruitful merchants have entered exchanging after a practical vocation in another field. Be that as it may, making progress in the business sectors is very not quite the same as making progress in different occupations. The business sectors don't reward the character qualities that are created and compensated in various professions. Do you have character qualities that have stretched you beyond on the planet, however, may not advance you beyond in the business sectors? If you do, you may need to chip away at changing a portion of these characteristics to be an active broker.

Let us audit a portion of the character characteristics that may not help exchange. Take congruity, for instance. When stirring your way up the professional bureaucracy, it is indispensable to have the option to see how you fit into the association. One should precisely see what their bosses see as the bearing for the organization, whether or not one concurs with this course or not. Congruity is frequently remunerated over autonomous reasoning and autonomy. If you have worked in a corporate setting, you are most likely mindful of how everybody appears to loathe the individual who is continually addressing cooperative choices and appears to self-advance his thoughts to the detriment of the gathering.

Conversely, congruity is a constraint as opposed to advantage with regards to exchanging. In a perfect world, merchants look just inside themselves for definitive answers. They don't depend on the assessments of others, are doubtful of winning conclusions, and ceaselessly attempt to locate another exchanging plan before every other person so that they can beat the group, as opposed to tail them.

Identified with congruity is amiability. In numerous occupations, individuals work with others. They should coexist with others, see their necessities, and once in while respect the requirements of others to the detriment of their own needs. Fruitful dealers, conversely, are rough individualists. Ordinarily, friendliness, and exchanging don't blend. A broker must settle on free choices, which, once more, implies glimpsing inside themselves to locate the correct answers. It might likewise mean investing much energy alone considering the business sectors and getting ready for exchanges, as opposed to spending time with others (which is additionally valid for some different occupations). Dealers must locate the correct harmony between satisfying the need.

9.6 Bullish and Bearish Candlesticks Pattern:

Candlestick Basics

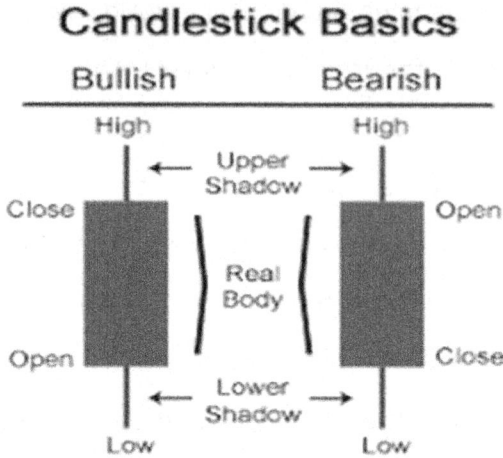

Figure 15: Candlestick Chart Basic Concept
Source 15: Own Sourced

Candlesticks are a kind of budgetary graph for following the development of protections. They have their starting points in the hundreds of years old Japanese rice exchange and have advanced into cutting edge cost charting. Some financial specialists discover them more outwardly engaging than the standard bar diagrams and the value activities simpler to decipher. Candles are so named because the rectangular shape and lines on either end take after a flame with wicks. Every candle, for the most part, speaks to one day of valuable information about a stock. After some time, the candles bunch into conspicuous examples that financial specialists can use to settle on purchasing and selling choices.

9.6.1 Bullish Candlestick Patterns

After some time, gatherings of everyday candles fall into glaring examples with unmistakable names like three white troopers, foreboding shadow spread, Hammer, morning star, and deserted child, to name only a few.3 Patterns structure over a time of one to about a month and are a wellspring of significant understanding into a stock's future value activity. Before we dive into individual bullish candle designs, note the accompanying two standards:

Optimistic inversion examples should shape inside a downtrend. Something else, it is anything but an encouraging example, yet a continuation design.

Most bullish inversion designs require bullish affirmation. They should be trailed by an upside value move, which can come as a long empty candle or a hole up and be joined by high exchanging volume. This affirmation ought to be seen inside three days of the example.

The bullish inversion examples can additionally be affirmed through different methods for customary specialized examination—like pattern lines, force, oscillators, or volume markers—to reaffirm purchasing pressure.

100

There are a large number of candle designs that show a chance to buy. We will concentrate on five bullish candle designs that give the most grounded inversion signal.

1. The Hammer or the Inverted Hammer:

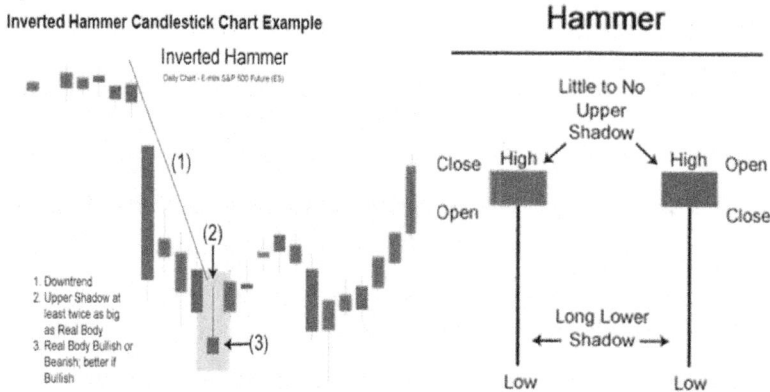

Figure 16: Inverted Hammer Candlestick Chart Sample

Source 16: Tutorial on How to Trade the Inverted Hammer Signal| Hammer and inverted hammer candlestick patterns; Forex Expert - youtube.com

The Hammer is a bullish inversion design, which flags that a stock is approaching base in a downtrend. The body of the light is short with a more extended lower shadow, which is an indication of vendors driving costs lower during the exchanging meeting, just to be trailed by stable purchasing strain to end the session on a higher close.

Before we hop in on the bullish inversion activity, in any case, we should affirm the upward pattern by watching it intently for the following hardly any days. The inversion should likewise be approved through the ascent in the exchanging volume.

The Inverted Hammer additionally shapes in a downtrend and speaks to a possible pattern inversion or backing. It's indistinguishable from the Hammer aside from the more drawn out upper shadow, which demonstrates purchasing pressure after the initial cost, trailed by extensive selling pressure, which anyway wasn't sufficient to bring the price down underneath its initial worth. Once more, bullish affirmation is required, and it can come as a long empty candle or a hole up, joined by a substantial exchanging volume.

2. The Bullish Engulfing:

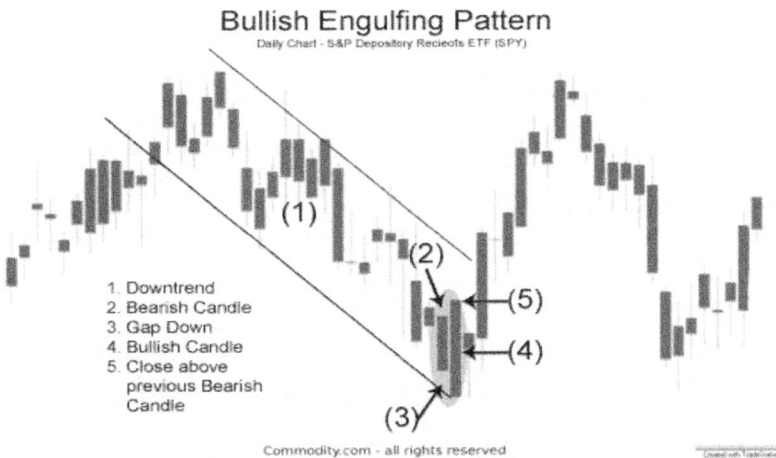

1. Downtrend
2. Bearish Candle
3. Gap Down
4. Bullish Candle
5. Close above previous Bearish Candle

Figure 17: Bullish Engulfing Candlestick Patterns

Source 17: How to Master the Bullish Engulfing Pattern; commodity.com

102

The Bullish Engulfing design is a two-light inversion design. The second flame totally 'inundates' the whole body of the first, regardless of the length of the tail shadows. The Bullish Engulfing diagram shows up in a downtrend and is a blend of one dim flame followed by a more significant empty light. On the second day of the example, value opens lower than the past low, yet purchasing pressure pushes the cost up to a more elevated level than the past high, coming full circle in a conspicuous success for the purchasers. It is fitting to enter a long position when the value moves more senior than the top of the second inundating light. (Guru, 2020)[17]

There are many bearish inversion designs. We have chosen to tight the field by selecting a couple of the most famous examples of nitty-gritty clarifications. For a total rundown of bearish and bullish inversion designs, see Greg Morris' book, Candlestick Charting Explained. The following are a portion of the critical bearish inversion designs, with the number of candles required in brackets. (Nordstrom)[18]

---

[17] Guru, F. (2020, February 25). The Engulfing Candlestick Pattern and how to trade it. Retrieved from From
Media: http://frommedia.com/the-engulfing-candlestick-pattern-and-how-to-trade-it/
[18] Nordstrom, J. (n.d.). The Bullish Engulfing Candle Trading Strategy. Retrieved from Trading Walk:
https://tradingwalk.com/bullish-engulfing-pattern

It is essential to recall the accompanying rules identifying with bearish inversion designs:

- Most examples need further bearish affirmation;
- Bearish inversion examples should shape inside an upturn;
- Different parts of specialized examination ought to be utilized, too.

9.6.2 Bearish Candlesticks:

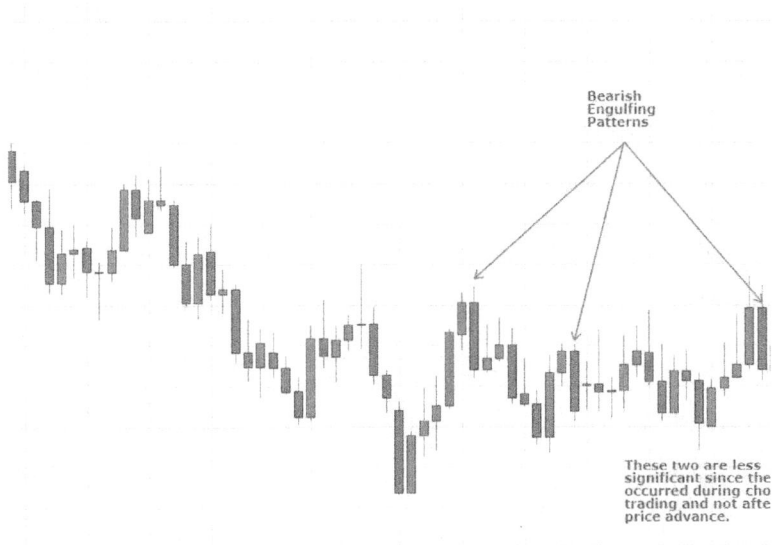

Figure 18: Bearish Engulfing Candlestick Patterns

Source 18: Bearish Engulfing Pattern Definition and Tactics; Investopedia

Bearish inversion examples can frame with at least one candle; most require bearish affirmation. The good inversion shows that selling pressure overpowered purchasing pressure for at least one day.

However, it stays hazy whether supported selling or absence of purchasers will keep on pushing costs lower. Without affirmation, a significant number of these examples would be viewed as nonpartisan and just show a potential opposition level, best case scenario. The bearish statement implies further drawback finish, for example, a hole down, long dark candle, or high-volume decrease. Since candle designs are present moment and generally successful for one fourteen days, the bearish affirmation should go in close vicinity to 1-3 days.

Time Warner (TWX) progressed from the upper fifties to the low seventies in under two months. A long-legged Doji trailed the long white candle that took the stock over 70 in late March in the harami position. A second long-legged Doji quickly followed and showed that the upswing was starting to tire. The foreboding shadow spread (red oval) expanded these doubts, and bearish affirmation was given by the long dark candle (red bolt).

These are only three potential strategies. A few brokers may incline toward shorter upturns and qualify protections that are exchanging over their 10-day EMA. Characterizing measures will rely upon your exchanging style, time skyline, and individual inclinations.

9.7 Other Technical Analysis:

Candles give a fantastic way to distinguish momentary inversions, yet ought not to be utilized alone. Different parts of specialized examination can and ought to be fused to build the power of bearish inversion designs.

9.7.1 Energy:

Use oscillators to affirm debilitating strength with bearish inversions. Negative divergences in MACD, PPO, Stochastics, RSI, Stoch RSI, or Williams %R shows are debilitating energy and can expand the vigor of a bearish inversion design. Also, bearish moving standard hybrids in the PPO and MACD can give affirmation, just as trigger line hybrids for the Slow Stochastic Oscillator.

9.7.2 Cash Flows:

Use volume-based pointers to survey selling pressure and affirm inversions. On Balance Volume (OBV), Chaikin Money Flow and the Accumulation/Distribution Line can be utilized to spot negative divergences or just excessive selling pressure.

Indications of expanded selling weight can improve the power of a bearish inversion design.

For those that need to make it one stride further, each of the three angles could be joined for a definitive sign. Search for a bearish candle inversion in protections exchanging close to obstruction with debilitating energy and indications of expanded selling pressure. Such signals would be moderately uncommon, yet could offer better than expected benefit potential.

9.8 The Engulfing Candlestick Pattern and Gaps:

Overwhelming candle Pattern comprises of two candles. It shows a stable bullish or bearish inversion assumption of the market. This example is all the more remarkable when it shows up close to help or obstruction. In bullish immersing design, a green light should overwhelm the red flame. The green flash can open at hole down and immerse the red, or it can begin at the cost of past shut light and inundate it completely.

9.9 The Development of Bullish Engulfing Candle:

The development of the Bullish Engulfing Candle appears as though a Green flame completely covers the assortment of earlier day red light.

As appeared in the image beneath, the green light can begin with a hole down. Additionally, it can open at a similar cost of earlier day close, yet it must cover the full assortment of former day flame.

Indeed, a bullish immersing design is hammer light. At the point when we consolidated the two candles with the assistance of mixing flame approach, we get a sled arrangement as appeared in the image beneath.

The bearish immersing flame arrangement seems as though a red light opened with a hole up; however, wholly secured the group of earlier day Green flame and close beneath the collection of former day flame. Bearish immersing can likewise begin with more initial day shut cost, yet it must overwhelm a full group of earlier day red light. The accompanying picture shows both with hole up and at value development.

Indeed, an overwhelming bearish flame is falling starlight when we use mixing light methodology. As appeared in the image beneath, the two candles are included and come about flash was a meteorite.

The accompanying picture shows a case of Bearish overwhelming example. As should be obvious, the cost opened with the hole up, and it ultimately secured the earlier day flame body. Additionally, it shut underneath the more initial day flame body. The red lines show the first daylight body.

As should be evident in the accompanying picture, the EURUSD visit is indicating an overwhelming bearish example, and we saw the market altered its course from bullish to bearish.

The accompanying photo shows the upbeat immersing design on the GBPNZD day by day outline. As should be obvious, the market opened with the hole down; however, it shut over the earlier day flame body. In this manner, it set off the opinion of bullishness, and the market went towards the north.

109

As examined before, the overwhelming example is falling star or sled design. So, the exchanging technique would be the same. Dealers can trigger purchase or sell requests after the overwhelming light is framed and shut while finishing covering the past body. The stop misfortune will go underneath or over the previous high. As appeared in the accompanying picture, the stop misfortune is beneath the dark specked line, and that is low of this climb

Correspondingly, additionally, note these arrangements are happening at the opposition level. Thus, the market will concur that overwhelming candle design is a positive inversion sign, and it is critical to check whether that shows up close to opposition or bolster level. Remember to check Hammer Candle, Shooting Star, Piercing flame, and Dark Cloud light arrangement design that happens increasingly regularly, and brokers love them!

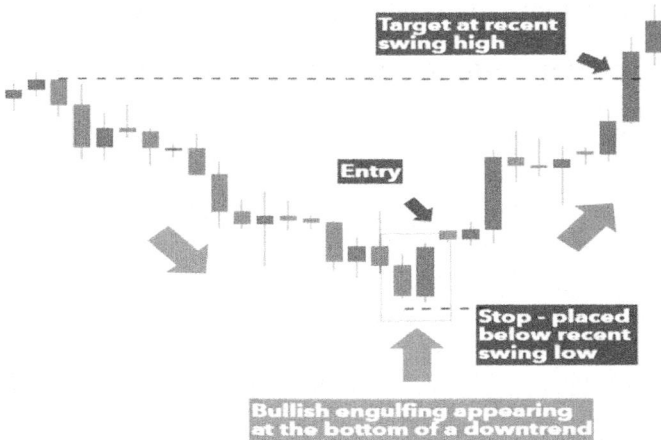

Figure 19: The development of bullish engulfing candle

Source 19: Own sourced

9.10 How to Isolate the Emotional Components from the Trading Decision?

At the point when your well-deserved cash is on the line, being balanced isn't simple.

In a perfect situation, a speculator ought to consistently "purchase low and sell high," however things don't generally work that way, and market elements frequently end up being more confounded than we anticipate that they should be.

A typical broker's day is troubled with a few enthusiastic highs and lows – certainty and uncertainties. With portfolio speculations fluctuating in cost continually, there's seldom when you don't have a specific feeling floating over you. Furthermore, controlling these feelings is actually what's expected to abstain from settling on choices that steer you off course.

Here are four activities to assist you with shielding your enthusiastic pendulum from influencing a lot during your exchanging day.

9.10.1 Recognize and Isolate:

Segregate feelings; the first and most significant activity is to recognize the emotions you're encountering. You simply made a significant benefit on a deal, and it is enticing you to go for additional, or the everyday misfortune sum has gotten over your head. You need to make only one benefit for the afternoon – STOP! Try not to let the feelings overwhelm you. Recognize and recognize them, and once you do, attempt to confine yourself from them. This is what you can do:

- Recall on past mix-ups made by contributing genuinely
- Redirect your consideration regarding the statistical data points of the interest being referred to and decide if it is worth the publicity.
- Leave your work area and go out for a walk. This will allow you to recompose yourself and clear your head.

9.10.2 Train Yourself

It is imperative to have objectives and an ensuing arrangement to accomplish them. These objectives may change additional time with the variances in showcase elements, and the method may require modifications as needs are, yet one thing stays steady all through – you DO NOT falter from your plan.

On the off chance that your policy says your permitted ten exchanges for the day, do whatever it takes not to surpass that. On the off chance that the arrangement says you quit exchanging after three continuous misfortunes, ensure you do. This will assist you with keeping the allurement, and the typical passionate floods leveled out, and help you with increasing higher authority over your choices.

9.10.3 Try not to React Immediately:

Frequently a quick response originates from an incautious inclination. It is essential to permit sufficient opportunity to pass and have a reasonable psyche and be fit for settling on the right choice. "Retribution Trading" is one of the most widely recognized responses to a misfortune; in the same way as other others, this will prompt lament and could prompt further indiscreet responses.

Have a go at expelling yourself from your workplace (my most loved is to step outside for natural air and open environment) for in any event 5 minutes. During that time, give a valiant effort to consider something inconsequential to contributing. At the point when you are feeling less incautious, come back with an unmistakable head to move toward the circumstance. Keep in mind; this staggering inclination is brief!

9.10.4. Avoid the Media:

It is normal to feel excited about potential gainful speculation and rush into the choice of getting it even at more significant expenses because the media says it will perform well. In any case, it regularly demonstrates to have the contrary result for financial specialists. To ensure you don't let the "follow the pioneer" attitude ruin you, search for energetic realities, figures, and investigation that gives healthy thinking to the speculation. Try not to depend on the expression of the media!

While we may think it is anything but challenging to beat feelings throughout contributing – it's more complicated than one might expect. You have to continue reminding yourself about the way that passionate contributing regularly prompts wrong choices at an inappropriate time. You're here to search for high likelihood approaches to bring in cash, not miss out on potential returns because of indiscreet choices.

10. Money Management:

Successful money management the executives is critical in the cutting-edge lives in which we lead today. Assuming responsibility for your funds and getting your budgetary life altogether, shortly, is of most extreme significance. I unequivocally and honestly accept that on the off chance that you have significant funds set up, you can give greater cause, add to the ummah more and have a decent existence.

We should all undertaking to have the proper personal satisfaction and focus on the best in all that we do. It is obviously about having an equalization, yet we have to perceive that many regarded friends were monetarily steady and were, in this way, ready to support the ummah. The ummah needs to have specialists, able business people, and individuals who have a decent establishing in the fund.

Along these lines by having exceptional monetary abilities and being acceptable with cash will permit us to have command over our life, empower us to have choices, and to likewise carry on with an existence of commitment. Anyway, dealing with your cash like anything sets aside some effort to comprehend and to enhance.

10.1 Ten Essential Steps to Assist you in Dealing with your Money the Correct Way:

10.1.1 Think Before you Spend:

Be smart with your money and pay on your family as there is barakah in this. Anyway, when you're confronted with a spending choice, particularly an enormous buy choice, don't merely accept you can manage the cost of something. Affirm that you can really control the cost of it and that you haven't just dedicated those assets to another value. That implies utilizing your spending limit and the equalization in your checking and bank accounts to choose whether you can bear the cost of a buy. Recall that because the cash is there doesn't mean you can make the buy. You need likewise to consider every one of your bills and costs you'll need to pay before your next payday. It is indispensable that you think before you spend it!

10.1.2 Track your Spending and Use:

Little buys, to a great extent, include rapidly, and before you know it, you've overspent your financial limit. Begin following your spending to find places where you might be unwittingly overspending. Spare your receipts and compose your buys in a spending diary, ordering them so you can recognize territories where you make some hard memories holding your spending under control. There are numerous applications out there that can assist you with following your spending.

10.1.3 Have a Decent Spending Plan Set up:

Numerous individuals don't spend plans since they would prefer not to experience what they think will be an exhausting procedure of rattling off costs, including numbers, and ensuring everything lines up. In any case, in case you're terrible with cash, you genuinely don't have space for pardons with planning. If everything necessary to get your spending on target is a couple of hours working a financial limit every month, is there any good reason why you wouldn't do it?

Rather than focusing on the way toward making a spending limit, center around the worth that planning will bring to your life.

10.1.4 Add to Your Investment Funds Normally:

Saving cash into an investment account every month can assist you with building sound monetary propensities. You can even set it up, so the money is naturally moved from your financial records to your bank account. That way, you don't need to make sure to make the exchange. Being acceptable with cash takes practice. At the outset, you may not be accustomed to preparing and postponing buys until you can bear the cost of them. The more you make these propensities part of your day by day life, the simpler it is to deal with your cash, and the happier your funds will be. Start with little commitments, and before you know it, it will have a significant effect!

10.1.5 Set Something Aside for Any Enormous Buys:

The capacity to defer delight will go far in helping you be better with cash. At the point when you put off tremendous bargains, instead of giving up progressively significant basics or putting the purchase on a Visa, you allow yourself to assess whether the buy is essential and much more opportunity to think about costs. In this manner, do everything in your self-control to put something aside for enormous bargains as you'll see that you will, at that point, value it more.

10.1.6 Set an Investment Funds Objective/Target:

A few people think that it's challenging to get inspired about sparing, yet it's frequently a lot simpler on the off chance that you set an objective.

Your initial step ought to be to have some crisis reserve funds (this is non-debatable) – you should have the cash to swear by on the off chance that you have a crisis, for example, an evaporator breakdown or if you can't work for some time. Attempt to get three months of costs in a simple or moment get to account. Try not to stress if you can't spare this straight away, yet save it as an objective to focus on.

The ideal approach to set aside cash is to pay some money into a bank account each month. When you've put aside your secret stash, potential investment funds objectives to consider may include: purchasing a vehicle without applying for a new line of credit, going on Hajj, taking a family occasion without stressing over the bills when you get back or in any event, having some additional cash to draw on while you're on maternity or paternity leave. Whatever you do, consistently have a few reserve funds for a stormy day!

10.1.7 Get Proficient Assistance if your Obligation Issues Become Genuine:

On the off chance that you've just missed charge card or credit installments or in case you're behind with purported 'need obligations,' for example, your lease, contract, vitality charges, Council charge or other at that point please accept exhortation from an obligation counsel noble cause straight away. On the off chance that you don't make a brief move, at that point, things can heighten, and the circumstance can undoubtedly detonate and aggravate things much.

I know numerous individuals who are in significant obligation, and this could have been handily kept away from if they looked for guidance and backing.

10.1.8 Figure out How to Organize Your Funds:

After your costs and pay, your objectives are probably going to have the most significant effect on how you dispense your investment funds. Make sure to recall long haul objectives as it's substantial that anticipating retirement doesn't take a secondary lounge to shorter-term needs. Learn how to organize your investment funds objectives, so you have an away from where to begin sparing. For instance, if you realize you're going to need to supplant your vehicle sooner rather than later, you could start taking care of cash for one at this point, whatever you do figure out how to live inside your methods!

10.1.9 Contribute your Investment Funds on the Off-Chance that you can:

On the off chance that your reserve funds begin to develop, you can contribute a portion of your capital.

It's an extraordinary method to ensure you'll have the option to live more easily sometime down the road. You can likewise make a venture arrangement dependent on your objectives and periods. There are halal alternatives accessible these days, for example, Wahid Invest, which is a one of a kind halal speculation stage.

10.1.10 Combine your Obligation and Attempt to dispose of it ASAP!

If you have the obligation, at that point, the principal activity is to get everything leveled out and take a shot at disposing of it. If you have Visa obligations, understudy credits, and different obligations, I hope to solidify them when you can. Once more, it's everything about finding a way to control your cash. There are obvious choices out there that permit you to consolidate a few uncollateralized debts, for example, charge cards, individual advances, and payday advances, into one bill as opposed to paying them separately.

On the off chance that you just have a solitary Visa obligation and are on a strict spending plan, have a go at playing, in any event, the base sum when you get the charge card bill. At that point, if your funds grant it, and you go over some more cash, attempt to make a similar installment half a month later. Have a go at keeping this installment cycle going until your obligation is completely paid off. On the off chance that conceivable by any means, at that point, make an arrangement to dispose of your debt. We ought to be monetarily stable, and we should have the option to deal with our accounts adequately!

10.2 Building and Fixing a Swing Trader Routine:

Are you additionally battling to discover an opportunity to set up an excellent exchanging routine other than working your standard day work, following your leisure activities, and investing energy with loved ones? You are not the only one. We know from direct experience that shuffling every one of our commitments while attempting to improve as a merchant is hard.

Setting up a superior exchanging routine and having the option to utilize your constrained time will have a significant distinction on your exchange. The issue is, 90% of all exchanging destinations just spotlight on the best way to pick sections and examine the most up to date markers, rather than discussing how to manufacture an expert and organized daily schedule around your own, day by day life.

On the off chance that your exchanging could require some structure and if you need to figure out how to consolidate all the things that are essential to you in your life, this article tells you the best way to accomplish only that.

When do you have time? A first appraisal

The first and most significant thing is to make a review of your own life. At what times would you say you are grinding away, when wouldn't you be able to check your outlines potentially and what amount of time do you truly have on your hands to exchange?

Let's assume seven days of an individual with ordinary day work. If you resemble a great many people, you will go through 35 – 50 hours out of each week grinding away. You presumably likewise participate in leisure activities after work (sports, companions, and so on) and take a break throughout the end of the week. What's more, although this seems like a bustling life as of now, it, as a rule, leaves sufficient opportunity to chip away at your exchanging aptitudes and discover time to exchange. A regular timetable of the average individual looks something like this. The white territories are typically spent staring at the TV, messing around, or doing other 'less significant' things. We'll get to that in a piece.

10.3 What is the methodology that accommodates your way of life?

Your exchanging approach must be picked with care. Not all exchanging styles are similarly useful for various ways of life, and by purposefully selecting the exchanging method that works out in the right way for your own life, you can fundamentally expand the chances of progress since you are bound to follow your exchanging schedule.

10.3.1 Alternative 1: Day Exchanging:

Day exchanging implies that you open and close your exchanges inside a couple of hours. Informal investors, for the most part, exchange the lower periods and have numerous transactions every day. In any case, being an everyday investor implies that you need to follow the business sectors when they are open effectively. For instance, a US-based merchant with a 9-5 occupation will, as a rule, experience issues day exchanging the US showcase since his average employment coincides when the US financial exchange is open and, in this way, he can't effectively follow what's going on in the live markets. In any case, a similar US dealer could decide to exchange the European, Asian and Australian meetings (or parts of it) after he returns home from work. Those are only two models of how considering the time zone you are in and your activity calendar, and afterward picking a fitting business sector can assist you with discovering approaches to consolidate individual life and exchanging. The timetable beneath shows how an informal investor could fit in exchanging time other than his 'normal life.' There is still a great deal of opportunity to get better. Later we will perceive how to utilize it successfully.

10.3.2 Alternative 2: Swing Exchanging:

Swing merchants, for the most part, exchange the higher periods, and they hold exchanges for a few days and here and there weeks. Consequently, swing brokers regularly don't sit before their screens throughout the day, yet just check their positions a couple of times during the day.

Thus, swing exchanging is frequently simpler to join with a 9-5 occupation and different obligations since you need less 'screen-time.' A swing merchant would, in this manner need $1 - 2$ hours each morning before he gets the chance to work to check his exchanges, examine and deal with his positions if fundamental and plan his thoughts. After work, he does likewise: he goes through 2 hours to go over his posts, breaks down them, screens the business sectors, plays out an examination, and plans his next exchanging day.

This is the thing that isolates the gainful from the losing merchant. The standard battling merchant closes down his foundation Friday evening when the business sectors are shutting and afterward revives it on Monday morning. The expert and genuine broker, then again, think about the worth end of the week time has. At the point when the business sectors are shut, the actual work for a merchant begins.

I locate that an astounding part of what sets up dealers for progress during the day is the thing that has happened the previous night. – Dr. Steinberger

At whatever point the market is shut (this additionally means your weekday night times), you can have the best effect in your exchange. A genuine dealer surveys his exchanges, breaks down the instruments he follows, composes and refreshes his exchanging plan, diaries his exchanges his exchanging diary, and sets himself up for the following day. Only doing this for 60 – an hour and a half consistently and following what we have recently said will change your exchanging past what you believe is conceivable. On the ends of the week, you should shut out more opportunities to take a shot at your exchanging abilities, thoroughly audit your past exchanging week, go over your exchanging diary again and play out an inside and out an investigation of the instruments and markets you are viewing. The table beneath shows how your week after week schedule could resemble.

Undertaking yourself five years into what's to come. Is it true that you are going to wish you had observed more TV or invested more energy at the bar, or would give up 2 hours every night merit coming nearer to your fantasy about turning into a full-time broker and afterward do all the things you always envisioned about?

10.4 The Fantasy of Screen-Time:

Dealers regularly talk about the idea of screen-time, and they accept that they need to go through a few hours every day, gazing at their graphs to turn out to be better brokers. Be that as it may, most brokers just arbitrarily flip through periods to chase for exchange signals, surf through gatherings to discover better frameworks, or talk with different dealers. The latter is likewise not satisfactory about what they are doing.

Practice doesn't make great. Just impeccable careful discipline brings about promising results. – Vince Lombardi

Rather than burning through your valuable time, use it astutely. The watchword is a conscious practice. We challenge you to stop what you have been doing and begin applying an increasingly proper methodology. We have referenced before that keeping an exchanging plan, assessing your exchanges, keeping an exchanging diary, and following an organized method will dramatically affect your trade. Is it accurate to say that you are worn out on not seeing any outcomes? Possibly it's an ideal opportunity to have a go at something new.

10.5. Real stock marketing trading strategies

Without the correct information, exchanging can be overpowering under the most favorable circumstances, so what would you be able to do to lessen your hazard and guarantee you have a high likelihood of achievement. While there is not a viable alternative for appropriate instruction with regards to exchanging the business sectors, if you don't have the information to benefit reliably, I suggest these five top securities exchange systems.

Purchase quality over amount

About putting away your well-deserved money, it is essential to purchasing quality blue-chip shares consistently. It doesn't make a difference whether you own one offer or a thousand suggestions; it's the nature of the offers you own that matters.

On the off chance that you make 10 percent on 1,000 offers in a penny repulsive stock or 10 percent on 100 proposals in a sizeable blue-chip organization, you have still made 10 percent. The likelihood of bringing in cash is a lot higher with quality blue-chip shares since they are progressively fluid and better oversaw, along these lines, financial specialists have more sureness of having the option to enter or leave a stock uninhibitedly.

Albeit as opposed to mainstream thinking, on the off chance that you put resources into top-quality stocks and adopt a generally safe orderly strategy to contributing over the long haul, the vast majority of the time you will accomplish far better yields than if you attempt to beat the market by picking the following blast stock or putting resources into penny dreadful. This way of thinking is frequently disregarded because, as people, we accept we can beat the measurements. In any case, the reality of the situation is that most financial specialists wind up, turning into an analysis. As I generally state, with regards to putting resources into shares, it isn't the amount you make on anyone venture that makes you well off; it is the amount you don't lose after some time.

Set cutoff points

Regardless of whether we are in a bull or bear showcase, the most significant single misstep individuals make in the financial exchange isn't selling a stock that is in benefit or not selling when it is in a misfortune. At the point when I present to crowds, I generally ask who realizes when to purchase a stock, and obviously, the more substantial part say indeed, however, when I ask who understands when to sell a stock, not very many lift their hands.

This is because, in my experience, people center 80 to 90 percent of their time searching for what to purchase as opposed to overseeing what they own and working out when to sell.

The fundamental motivation behind why individuals don't sell shares they are losing cash on or shares that are in benefit is a result of their feelings. Sadly, individuals are frightened of passing up a great opportunity, especially if a stock is in misfortune, as they trust it will turn and exchange back up, which isn't generally the situation.

In this manner, it is generally suggested that you set cutoff points by utilizing a leave technique if a stock doesn't proceed true to form or on the off chance that it has run its course with the goal that you lock in the benefits. While a great many people possibly stress when the stock they own is going down, if you set cutoff points on dealing with your hazard, you will be increasingly loose about what unfurls in the market. Given this, it is suggested that you should set a stop misfortune before you enter an exchange.

Try not to theorize

This announcement remains constant with regards to the financial exchange, as there are just two things you can control, and that is when to get in and when to get out because once you contribute, the market is in charge.

Accordingly, I generally prescribe trusting that the market will accomplish something before you settle on a choice as opposed to hypothesizing on what it may do. The same number of have encountered, on the off chance that you exchange without the correct information, the market will inevitably take your cash. However, if you increase appropriate training, utilizing dominant financial exchange exchanging systems, it will give you the certainty to enter and leave transactions with the goal that you don't need to estimate since it is much better to exchange on affirmation, instead of theory.

Bull and bear remaining on a paper

Another dangerous mix-up individuals will, in general, make when they begin in the financial exchange is to buy programming trusting it will assist them with their exchanging choices about which stocks to purchase and sell. While on a superficial level, this sounds extraordinary, awfully many spend their well-deserved money on costly programming bundles that guarantee wealth from next to no exertion or capital, just to find this is necessarily false.

There's a well-known adage, 'what a shrewd man does first and foremost, a moron does at long last.'

At the point when I get some information about their exchanging procedure and what financial exchange was exchanging useful techniques, I find that such a large number of having followed the way of the 90 percent who neglect to bring in cash in the securities exchange, and barely any observe their errors. To be sure, the 90 percent who do come up short, neglect to design appropriately because they don't increase legitimate training.

Use alert with showcasing organizations

A great deal of securities exchange training is advanced by organizations who are more engaged with promoting than giving quality instruction. Their propensity is to paint an excessively positive perspective on exchanging by demonstrating financial specialists how much cash they can make, however never genuinely giving a realistic view on the amount they can lose by applying their exchanging systems. My recommendation is to do your exploration and ensure you can qualify and evaluate all that they state.

With regards to the securities exchange, having the correct mentality is essential to your drawn-out progress. So be clear about what you need to accomplish and why, and focus on it.

An active merchant submits time and cash to building up the correct information and aptitudes and picking up involvement with the market. Things being what they are, would you say you are one of the 90 percent, or would you say you are unique? Being various methods, you have the establishments to turn into an incredible dealer since you have figured out how to apply the correct financial exchange exchanging systems that work in any economic situation. My best ten offer tips will give you some incredible bits of knowledge on the securities exchange, just as scatter various legends and misinterpretations in the market that keep numerous away from contributing.

10.6. Risk cases in stock market

In stock trading, there is a stable connection between hazard and return. More noteworthy, the risk, more noteworthy the arrival by and large! In money-related phrasing hazards, the board is the way toward recognizing and evaluating the danger and afterward creating techniques to oversee and limit the equivalent while expanding the profits.

Each speculation requests a specific measure of hazard, and for a financial specialist to expect this hazard, he must be rewarded appropriately.

This remuneration is through something many refer to as the hazard premium or virtually the bonus. Risk is hence fundamental to securities exchanges or contributing because, without the chance, there can be no increases. Capable financial specialists utilize securities exchange chance administration techniques to limit the hazard and boost the rise.

In money related markets, there are commonly two sorts of hazards; first, the Market hazard and second the Inflation chance. Market hazard results from an opportunity in increment or diminishing of money related markets. The other risk, for example, the Inflation or the buying power chance outcomes from rising and fall of costs of merchandise and ventures after some time.

The expansion hazard is a significant thought in long haul ventures, whereas the market chance is increasingly pertinent temporarily. It is the market chance that can be overseen and controlled partly. The swelling hazard can't be controlled.

Certain procedures can be utilized to relieve the hazard in a securities exchange. The systems are as per the following:

Follow the pattern of the market:

This is one of the demonstrated techniques to limit chances in a financial exchange. The issue is that it is hard to spot slants in the market, and patterns change quickly.

A market pattern may last a single day, a month or a year, and again transient patterns work inside long-haul patterns.

Portfolio Diversification:

Another valuable hazard the board system in the securities exchange is to enhance your risk by putting resources into a portfolio. In a collection, you strengthen your venture to a few organizations, divisions, and resource classes. There is a likelihood that while the market estimation of specific speculation diminishes, that of the other may increment. Shared Funds are one more intends to broaden the effect.

Stop Loss:

Stop misfortune or trailing device is one more gadget to watch that you don't lose cash should the stock go far a fall. In this methodology, the speculator has the choice of exiting if a specific stock falls underneath one particular indicated limit. Self-control is one more choice utilized by individual speculators to sell when the stock falls underneath one particular level or when there is a precarious fall.

Ask warren buffet, the best financial specialist ever, what is your recommendation to speculators, and he says, 'don't lose cash!' But securities exchange means hazard, and luckily there are sufficient techniques for an insightful speculator to defend his cash and guarantee gain.

A cautious and timely exercise of these alternatives encourages you to see the hazard in question. Game-changing strategies
In principle, the administration goes about as ligament to keep the interests of organizations and the general population from pounding on one another. The administration steps in when business is jeopardizing people in general and appears to be reluctant to control itself. By and by, the administration tends to over-administer. Enactment builds a clear picture of the significance of the legislature, just as furnishing the individual congressmen with exposure. These unusual motivating forces lead to a much more administrative hazard than is genuinely fundamental.

10.7. Risk management in Stock Trading

A stock exchange isn't as simple and straightforward as it sounds from its definition. The offer market has a genuinely capricious nature. Thus, there are different dangers and uncertainly engaged with the stock business. The elevated level of hazard encompassing stock exchanging propels individuals to mull over this business. Notwithstanding that, stock dealers are required to pay weighty aggregates of cash as business charges to the bank of financier firms. It's a given that stock exchange isn't for the timid.

Compelling Strategies of Stock Trading

Regardless of the unpredictable idea of the business, stock exchanging can prompt momentous budgetary achievement. Stock dealers utilize various systems to handle the complexities of stock trading and expand benefits. The following is a rundown of 4 such techniques.

1) Day Trading

In this type of stock exchange, stocks are purchased and sold inside a 24-hour term so that before the finish of that period, the stock merchant doesn't have any share close by. Day time stock merchants sell an offer at whatever point another portion of comparable worth is bought. The benefit and misfortune are dictated by the contrast between the deal cost and the purchasing cost of the offer. As referenced previously, the securities exchange is a significant violent spot where prices can go here and there surprisingly fast. Thus, stockbrokers' resort to day time exchanging to abstain from bringing about any misfortunes because of uncommon short-term changes in the financial exchange.

2) Swing Trading

Swing exchanging includes clutching stocks from anyplace between several days to a little while.

Swing dealers are worried about shares that are purchased and sold as often as possible. These stocks will go in general sway between a public high and a low extraordinary. At the point when these stocks are at the flat finish of their worth, stock dealers get them and sell them when their costs rise once more.

3) Value contributing

In the stock exchange, esteem contributing is a system utilized by stockbrokers to purchase shares that can increment in esteem after some time. These offers are fundamentally organization stocks that are at first under-estimated. When it arrives at its most extreme worth, the stock dealers auction them for a huge benefit.

4) Growth contributing

Development contributing is one more method of winning benefits in the field of a stock exchange. At the point when organizations bear signs of a substantial development rate, their offers are purchased by stockbrokers. Rather than esteem financial specialists, development speculators buy shares that are on the costly side. In any case, as indicated by their estimations, these offers are the ones that will proceed to be worth very much more than what they paid for it. The quicker the organization develops, the snappier the estimation of the stock ascents.

Stock exchanging is a thrill ride. Brokers should be on the alarm consistently to have any expectation of becoming famous in the offer market. They should be pioneers to be useful here. Everything comes down to consummate planning and a tad of karma.

10.8. The best time frame for swing trading

One inquiry that new dealers have is what the best periods for examination are when you are swing exchanging.

There is some exchanging technique to get a known time frame for swing trading. The quick and easy answer is a multi-time period examination. The multi-time allotment examination is crucial to anybody's exchanging investigation. Regardless of if you are day exchanging, swing trading, or in any event, contributing and utilizing technical.

Pattern Direction Identification
Week by week and day by day outlines:

About the period investigation, it is consistently amusing to begin at a more significant period. Something progressively reached out to see the bigger image of the market and to recognize the general pattern. At TRADE PRO institute, we like to utilize week after week to show us the general bearing of the stock or record being referred to.

The intensity of an outlined period down to a littler time allotment, for example, every day. On the off chance that once you drop down in periods, you can focus on the exchange area and follow the miniaturized scale pattern with more accuracy.

In the wake of having recognized the general week by week pattern, we know what direction the stock is going, and we can start to break down the situation being referred to. On the off chance that the pattern is robust to the upside or drawback, we may search for a pullback area to jump on the design and brave it. If the model appears as though it's concluding dependent on technical, backing, opposition, or volume, we may start to qualify a blur.

It's imperative to remember that now the total of what we have is a thought. Each exchange should begin with an idea. In light of that thought, we proceed with our exchanging plan and start to assemble a significant trade.

Now, we move down to the everyday outline to encourage the investigation. We will, at that point, distinguish, are we in an essential move in the pattern course or a therapeutic movement against the pattern. This will, at that point, assist us with pinpointing an increasingly thin zone of intrigue that has been searched for exchange sections. This is the thing that called the smaller scale pattern from the general move that found week after week.

On the off chance that the smaller scale pattern concurs with the general design, regardless of whether it's up or down. We may have qualified a more drawn out term exchange if the two plans are pointing a similar way. Furthermore, they are allowing us the chance to get a more significant move.

Be that as it may, there are cases in which the smaller scale pattern is the other way of the more extended term pattern. This might be viewed as a more modest scale pattern blur and a shorter length exchange opportunity. When this exchange is finished, the smaller scale pattern may have pulled back only enough for brokers to hop on the general pattern's side and ride a more extended exchange.

Notice that up until now, exchanges haven't made — it is all simply cycle and pattern investigation, with the advantage of distinguishing an objective section region for my swing exchanging technique. So, there you have it, a nitty-gritty clarification on the most proficient method to recognize and follow a pattern, and further drill down into section zones and executions. At the point when it is wholly said and done, a swing exchanging technique is the most significant part, trailed by your order in executing it.

Figure 20: Uptrend on the daily and weekly chart

Source 20: Own Sourced

When you have your guidelines, you can utilize the data above to assist you with burning through various graph time spans to stick point your entrance with laser exactness. There is nobody best period for swing exchanging, yet instead the multi-time span examination to assist you with recognizing the passage dependent on a top-down specialized investigation.

11.FAQ's

Q1. Why is Swing Trading thought about the best exchanging style?

Ans. It gives you the intensity of snappy benefits in only a couple of days or weeks without clinging to stock more extended term. Longer-term exchange is commonly appropriate for retirement accounts. Those of us looking for money on a month to month premise need more turnover and benefits. Day exchanging is a considerably increasingly present moment, yet your chances of progress are a lot of lower. Swing trading is the better of the two universes by permitting stock to move a productive way in a short measure of time without the enormous high points and low points of long term or day exchanging.

Q2. How regularly do you give new swing pick recommendations?

Ans. By and large, on average, around 2-3 new picks are given every month as current picks hit their benefit target. A ton of our individuals would state one pick seven days is adequate. If we are posting new picks all the more frequently, that is a decent sign that our proposals are making benefits quick!

Q3. Should I be a U.S. inhabitant to exchange your swing stock picks?

Ans. Although our stock picks are organizations recorded on US-based trades, you can live anyplace on the planet and exchange our picks. It will be ideal if you affirm with your dealer positively.

Q4. How huge of an exchanging account do I should be useful?

Ans. We recommend at least only $500 for subsidizing an exchanging account. Any less indeed doesn't permit you to exchange enough offers for each pick. Keep in mind, swapping - at least two open picks allow equalization and assurance on the off chance that one of the picks doesn't proceed true to form.

Q5. Do you place the exchanges for me?

Ans. No. We don't approach your assets or representative record - nor do we deal with any exchanges or cash. You are liable for setting the recommended exchanges with your intermediary and afterward leaving the transaction at the proposed cost, or whenever you wish. Keep in mind; our exchanges are proposals dependent on a higher likelihood of achievement. You are liable for any misfortunes brought about.

Q6. Will I get a discount if I drop my participation early or lose cash on an exchange?

Ans. No, yet you most likely won't lose cash if you follow our swing picks. Nonetheless, as we expressed above, there are things that we don't control, for example, a dependable web association and the communication among you and your dealers exchanging stage. We likewise do not affect the course of any stock. You may drop coming month to month participation rebills at whenever yet we don't give discounts for unused time. Your part's region access will terminate toward the finish of your latest multi-day charging period.

Q7. Do I have to hazard genuine cash before I begin exchanging your swing picks?

Ans. Not. Simply become a part and follow our picks for half a month. When you are confident and sure that we can make you cash, at that point, you can begin to hazard natural capital. We don't need anybody to chance good money until they are sure about their capacity to make an exchange and OK with our reliably gainful swing stock tips. On the off chance that you choose our picks are not for you, permanently drop your participation.

Q8. What sort of stocks do you pick?

Ans. The entirety of our stock picks exchange on the NYSE or NASDAQ trades. We by and large pick stocks valued somewhere in the range of $8 and $100 with adequate regular every day exchanging volume for good liquidity. We don't pick penny or OTC stocks. Those are commonly excessively unsafe.

Q9. How would you choose the best swing stocks to exchange?

Ans. Without parting with our exploration, privileged insights, have confidence, we just utilize freely accessible data, PC calculations, and different specialized and principal pointers to pick our picks. Our group cautiously picks each swing pick - each prepared to make a normal of a 5-10% move in the following scarcely any weeks. Exchanging, at any rate, two of the accessible picks will restore a verifiable normal of 10% when they hit the take benefit cost. A few picks have been known to climb almost 20%-well past the benefit target. At times a pick won't run the focus of the benefits before we choose to give a refreshed sell alert, yet we, despite everything, bring in cash. Our picks are, for the most part, totally lawful and prepared to make your benefits!

Q10. To what extent will I be in each exchange?

Ans. The term swing signifies exchanges that last somewhere in the range of 5 days to half a month. We are never in exchange for longer than 60 days. You permanently leave the transaction once our actual cost is reached, or in uncommon cases, the stop misfortune is reached. You can decide to exit whenever you wish. We like to get in and lock in our benefits at the earliest opportunity.

Q11. What number of swing stock tips do you give in the individual's zone portfolio?

Ans. The individual's just portfolio comprises of at any rate - 3 - swing stock exchange recommendations consistently. When a pick arrives at its benefit focus on, another pick is given to supplant it. There is always in any event 1-2 picks hanging tight for you to enter at whatever point you join. Since the business sectors are extremely delayed between Christmas day and New Year's Day, no new picks are included during that timeframe.

12. Conclusion:

After reading all of this, you may think you know it all, but it is important to understand that this was just the tip of the iceberg. There are tons of risks in thinking you know more than you actually do. Just because something hasn't happened before, does not mean that it can't or won't. Be ready to experience anything and constantly study and research more into Swing Trading, and even trading as a whole.

The topic of Swing Trading alone is so vast that trading as a whole doesn't even come close to it. You'll be studying certain things and concepts, and more confusing concepts will stem from them. No matter how much you learn, it is still never enough, and quite frankly, it never will be. You will constantly need to expand your knowledge, and since economic conditions are mostly unpredictable and constantly changing, new theories will arise for you to try to grab hold of. In trading, there will always be a winner and a loser. Your main aim should be to often remain on the winning side of the trade, in order to make a profit. But despite knowing all of this, and trying to act on the rules and strategies used by most traders, your trade decisions can still end up making you go into loss. Certain things you experience will go against that which you would have studied in theory.

Experience is the best teacher, and as you practice more and more, you will start making decisions that go in your favor, without even realizing it. It will become a skill like that of driving a car, and your subconscious knows what to do even if you aren't fully focused.

You learned many different trading techniques, more specifically in regard to Swing Trading, a form of Active Trading where positions are held for short periods of time. You were also able to compare between different types of Active Trading techniques to come to the conclusion that the best one is hands down Swing Trading, because it is the perfect balance between the two extremes, and it is also the least stress-inducing for beginners. In order to jump-start your trading skill, you also learned the basic step-by-step of how to analyze price index charts in order to make trading decisions; when to enter and when to exit, in such a way that you do not experience major losses. The different ways and techniques to reduce risk were briefly explained, as well. These terms will help you know what your broker is saying, in order to make sure they do not end up exploiting you.

The two main disciplines of trading were also explained to you, which remains the same for trading any asset, but we more specifically discussed it for Stocks. You learned the basic principles of Fundamental Analysis, and Technical Analysis was also introduced to you, along with the most relevant indicators for Swing Trading using the Technical Analysis. There is always a debate between traders about which method is more efficient and effective, but there is no such thing as the 'best.' Each analysis has different purposes and ideas behind it, and the one you should refer to solely depends on the type of trader you want to be. If you want to be a long-term investor, it is important to use the Fundamental Analysis to study how business and the economy will fluctuate to determine which stock you should buy. However, if you are a scalper or day-trader, it is smarter to refer to the Technical Analysis tools and software as they'll give you information quick and current price movements, which are what a day trader studies to make profits. As a Swing Trader, though, you should use a combination of the two disciplines, studying the trends being shown by the technical analysis, but also researching on the earnings of a company to determine if their stock value will change contrary to what the index charts depict. (WallStreetMojo)[19]

---

[19] WallStreetMojo. (n.d.). Fundamental Analysis vs. Technical Analysis. Retrieved from WallStreetMojo:

Trading Psychologies were also discussed. They refer to the mental state of a trader that helps to dictate whether the stock trade will be a success or a failure. How you can develop trading psychology in order to get the best profits was also explained to you, such as how to get yourself in the right mindset, how to learn to remain calm why trading, imagining different scenarios of wins and losses to make sure you don't let them get to your head. By developing the correct trading psychology, you can also influence your business plan, as with it, you remind yourself that all this is real money and that you should not take these decisions lightly by considering trading as a 'hobby' or 'side-project.' By mastering your emotions, you can learn to make more calm, collected, and informed decisions rather than hasty and hyper ones. It is also interlinked with the money management strategy in trading stocks, as you can help yourself understand that you may not be able to control where the market goes, but what you can control is how you invest in different stocks and what trading decisions you make. To manage your money properly, you were explained to start out with small risks so as to understand the trading market in a more accurate manner so as to limit your risks and hence losses.

---

https://www.wallstreetmojo.com/fundamental-analysis-vs-technical-analysis/

To conclude, do not hold a position unless you are prepared to sustain a total loss. All this information was to give you the basics of Swing Trading so that you determine whether trading is your forte or not and if it is then where and how you should begin. But when undertaking this in real life, it is suggested not to make any financial decision on trading without actually consulting a licensed professional who can help you make smart decisions, especially as a novice. Poor decisions can cause you to sustain large sums of losses, where you end up losing more than you invested. This book was very general in nature, and no matter how much you learn, the market can be quite unpredictable, going against all theories you learned because in the end, no one can truly predict the market, and any unforeseen event can suddenly break the trend completely, even against your favor.

Table of Figures:

Table of Tables:

Bibliography

Alvarez, A. (2018, September 14). *Game-Changing Marketing Trends You Need to Follow.* Retrieved from Relevance: Content Promotion News & Insights: https://www.relevance.com/game-changing-marketing-trends-you-need-to-follow-in-2018/

Bajpai, P. (2019, August 8). *Scalping vs. Swing Trading: What's the Difference?* Retrieved from Investopedia: https://www.investopedia.com/articles/active-trading/021715/scalping-vs-swing-trading.asp

Beattie, A. (2019, June 25). *The Pioneers of Technical Analysis.* Retrieved from Investopedia: https://www.investopedia.com/articles/financial-theory/10/pioneers-technical-analysis.asp

Comit. (2018, August 7). *Learn How to Make a Trading Plan.* Retrieved from Vantage Point Trading: https://vantagepointtrading.com/learn-how-to-make-a-trading-plan/

Curtis, G. (2020, April 4). *The Importance of Trading Psychology.* Retrieved from Investopedia: https://www.investopedia.com/articles/trading/02/110502.asp

Fuller, N. (2016, February 26). *Why Swing Trading Gives You The Best Chance to Succeed.* Retrieved from Learn to Trade the Market: https://www.learntotradethemarket.com/forex-trading-strategies/best-swing-trading-strategy

Gordon Scott, C., Michael Carr, C., & and Mark Cremonie, C. C. (2016). *Technical Analysis: Modern Perspectives.* The CFA Institute Research Foundation.

Guru, F. (2020, February 25). *The Engulfing Candlestick Pattern and how to trade it.* Retrieved from From Media: http://frommedia.com/the-engulfing-candlestick-pattern-and-how-to-trade-it/

Hayes, A. (2020, March 27). *Introduction to Technical Analysis Price Patterns.* Retrieved from Investopedia: https://www.investopedia.com/articles/technical/112601.asp

Hayes, A. (2020, April 22). *Moving Averages (MA).* Retrieved from Investopedia: https://www.investopedia.com/terms/m/movingaverage.asp

Hayes, A. (2020, March 16). *Technical Analysis.* Retrieved from Investopedia: https://www.investopedia.com/terms/t/technicalanalysis.asp#how-technical-analysis-is-used

Investopedia Staff. (2019, December 12). *An Introduction to Oscillators.* Retrieved from Investopedia: https://www.investopedia.com/articles/technical/070301.asp

Kuepper, J. (2019, August 19). *Risk Management Techniques for Active Traders.* Retrieved from Investopedia: https://www.investopedia.com/articles/trading/09/risk-management.asp

Majaski, C. (2020, Maech 27). *Day Trading vs. Swing Trading: What's the Difference?* Retrieved from Investopedia: https://www.investopedia.com/articles/active-trading/052815/pros-cons-day-trading-vs-swing-trading.asp

Nordstrom, J. (n.d.). *The Bullish Engulfing Candle Trading Strategy.* Retrieved from Trading Walk: https://tradingwalk.com/bullish-engulfing-pattern

PSG Staff. (n.d.). *Market Psychology Methods and Discipline of Trading Success.* Retrieved from PSG: https://www.psg.co.za/support/tutorials/market-psychology-method

Rolf. (n.d.). *How To Create A Trading Routine That Allows You To Reach Your Full Potential As A Trader.* Retrieved from EdgeWonk: https://edgewonk.com/how-to-create-a-trading-routine-that-allows-you-to-reach-your-full-potential-as-a-trader/

Segal, T. (2020, March 16). *Investopedia.* Retrieved from Fundamental Analysis: https://www.investopedia.com/terms/f/fundamentalanalysis.asp

Seth, S. (2019, June 25). *An Introduction to Price Action Trading Strategies.* Retrieved from Investopedia : https://www.investopedia.com/articles/active-trading/110714/introduction-price-action-trading-strategies.asp

WallStreetMojo. (n.d.). *Fundamental Analysis vs. Technical Analysis.* Retrieved from WallStreetMojo: https://www.wallstreetmojo.com/fundamental-analysis-vs-technical-analysis/

Wikipedia. (n.d.). *List of Stock Exchanges.* Retrieved from Wikipedia: https://en.wikipedia.org/wiki/List_of_stock_exchanges

Made in the USA
Columbia, SC
22 September 2020